Also by Peter Baxter:
Rhodesia: Last Outpost of the British Empire
France in Centrafrique: From Bokassa and Operation Barracuda to the days of the EUFOR
Selous Scouts: Rhodesian Counter-Insurgency Specialists
Mau Mau: The Kenyan Emergency, 1952–1960

Co-published in 2012 by:

Helion & Company Limited
26 Willow Road
Solihull
West Midlands
B91 1UE
England
Tel. 0121 705 3393
Fax 0121 711 4075
email: info@helion.co.uk
website: www.helion.co.uk

and

30° South Publishers (Pty) Ltd.
16 Ivy Road
Pinetown 3610
South Africa
email: info@30degreessouth.co.za
website: www.30degreessouth.co.za

Text © Peter Baxter, 2012
Photographs © as individually credited
Diagrams and maps by Genevieve Edwards
Aircraft colour profiles by William Marshall

Designed & typeset by Kerrin Cocks (kerrincocks@gmail.com)
Printed in the UK by Henry Ling Limited, Dorchester, Dorset
and in South Africa by Pinetown Printers (Pty) Ltd, Pinetown, KwaZulu-Natal

ISBN 978-1-920143-71-8 (South Africa)
ISBN 978-1-908916-23-5 (UK)

British Library Cataloguing-in-Publication Data
A catalogue record for this book is available from the British Library

Cover photo: A Buccaneer with an H2 bomb on the inner pylon and an EW pod on the outer pylon under the port wing. The H2 communications pod is under the starboard wing.

CONTENTS

GLOSSARY

AAA – anti-aircraft artillery. Triple A was the overall term used to describe the anti-aircraft guns that were employed in limited numbers by SWAPO, but extensively by the Angolan defence force. These guns covered the complete spectrum of Soviet-supplied weaponry and included: 12.7mm, 14.5mm, 20mm, 23mm, 37mm,* 57mm† (*This included the towed, twin-barrelled version that was probably the most widely employed and effective gun used in the entire campaign by either side, both in the ground-to-air and ground-to-ground mode. The four-barrelled, tracked version (Shilka) was also encountered. The 23mm cannons used by 32 Battalion, Koevoet and the SAAF were some of the many captured in operations over the years. Ironically, Angola probably became the biggest arms supplier to South Africa throughout the difficult years of arms boycotts. †These radar-guided guns were originally equipped with the Fire-can radar system and later updated with the flap-wheel version)

ACF – Active Citizen Force (territorials)

ACM – air combat manoeuvring, modern name for dogfighting

ACS – Air Combat School

ADF – automatic direction-finding navigational instrument which locks onto an NDB

AFB – air force base

AFCP – air force command post. The SAAF uses a system of command posts to efficiently command and control all the resources available to it. This includes aircraft, personnel, radars, air-defence systems and ground security squadron specialists with their dogs. An AFCP controls the air force involvement in its designated area of responsibility, which includes both ground and air battles. An FAC is subservient to an AFCP but handles all the equivalent operations, except it does not control the air battle

AGL – above ground level, the height in feet that the aircraft flies above the ground

AI – air interception

AK-47 – Automat Kalashnikov type 47, a standard Soviet-designed automatic assault rifle

Alouette III – single-engine light helicopter, the aerial workhorse of the Border War. In the trooper role it could carry a crew of two plus four soldiers, or two stretchers when used in the casevac role. In the offensive role as a gunship it carried a 20mm cannon firing out of the port side

alpha bomb – circular-shaped anti-personnel bomb weighing 6kg that when dropped by the Canberra from level flight gave a natural dispersion pattern. The bomb would strike the surface, activating the fusing mechanism and then bounce into the air to detonate about 6m above ground. This bomb was an improved version of that used by the Rhodesian Air Force, and 300 of them could be loaded into the bomb bay of a Canberra

ANC – African National Congress

ATC – Air Traffic Control

ATCO – Air Traffic Control Officer

avtur – aviation turbine fuel used in helicopter and fixed-wing jet-turbine engines

bandit – an aircraft identified as hostile

BDA – bomb damaged area

beacon – the cut-line designating the border between Angola and Owamboland stretched in a straight line 420km from the Cunene River in the west to the Kavango River in the east. Every 10km a concrete beacon was built to identify position in an otherwise featureless terrain. Beacon 16 was therefore 160km east of the Cunene River.

blue job – anybody serving in the air force (slang)

BM-21 – 122mm 40-tube multiple-rocket launcher, mounted on a Ural 375 truck, with a maximum range of 20,000m

Boere – a general-usage, normally derogatory term used by both SWAPO and the Angolans to describe the South African/SWATF security forces (from the Afrikaans *boer* meaning farmer)

bogey – an unidentified aircraft

bombshell – guerrilla tactic of splitting up during flight (slang)

Bosbok – single-piston engine, high-wing reconnaissance aircraft flown by two crew seated in tandem. In the bush war it was utilized in many roles, including visual and photographic reconnaissance, skyshout, pamphlet-dropping and Telstar

brown job – any soldier; variations were 'browns' or the more commonly pongos (slang)

Buccaneer – S-50 version of the British-built naval strike fighter; twin-engine, subsonic two-seater that could carry the full range of bombs plus AS-30 air-to-ground missiles

C-130 – four-engine turboprop heavy transport aircraft otherwise known as the Hercules. Used extensively throughout the bush war to support the actions of both ground-landing and air-dropping of personnel and freight (*see* Flossie)

C-160 – twin-engine tactical transport aircraft. Although limited in payload when compared to the C-130, it had the decided advantage of a larger-dimensioned freight compartment, allowing easier and quicker transporting of helicopters to the battle area. Known by NATO as the Transall it had the dubious distinction of being probably the most difficult and expensive aircraft to maintain in the inventory of the SAAF owing to the extreme difficulties imposed by the international arms embargo

Canberra – English Electric twin-engine, medium jet bomber, used as such and also in PR roles. Armament included alpha bombs, World War II-vintage 500lb and 1,000lb general-purpose bombs plus the South African-manufactured 120kg and 250kg GP and pre-fragmentation bombs

CAP – combat air patrol, the armed mission air-defence fighters fly to ensure safety of own aircraft in the battle area

CAS – close air support; aircraft supporting the ground forces in close proximity to the immediate battle line are termed to be giving CAS

casevac – casualty evacuation

Casspir – mine-protected, armoured personnel-carrier

CEP – centre of error probability, a mathematical method of determining the miss-distance of a number of weapons from the centre of a target

Cessna 185 – a single-engine, four-seater tail-dragger used in the communication, skyshout, pamphlet-dropping and Telstar roles, by day and night

CFS – Central Flying School

CO – commanding officer

COIN – counter-insurgency

contact – a firefight, i.e. when contact is made with the enemy

cut-line – the border between Angola and Owamboland, so named from the graded strip cut through the bush to demarcate the international border

D-30 – Soviet-built 122mm cannon with a range of 15,000m; also used in an anti-tank role

Dayton – the radio call sign of the radar station situated at AFB Ondangwa; all matters concerning air defence were the responsibility of Dayton

density altitude – aircraft aerodynamic and engine performance are adversely affected by high temperatures and low pressures. Because these criteria vary from airfield to airfield and on a daily basis, the term 'density altitude' is used to determine aircraft performance. At sea-level airfields in Europe during winter, a jet aircraft will produce more thrust and lift than it will at AFB Waterkloof, 5,000ft AGL, during the 30°C-plus temperatures of summer

dominee – padre (Afrikaans)

DR – dead reckoning, when navigating without electronic aids

DZ – drop zone

EATS – Empire Air Training Scheme

ECM/ECCM – electronic counter-measures/electronic-counter-counter-measures, part of EW (*see* EW)

ERU – explosive release unit, the device which ensures clean separation of bombs from the carrying aircraft

EW – electronic warfare; covers all aspects of warfare involving use of the electro-magnetic spectrum

FAC – Forward Air Controller

FAPA – *Força Aérea Popular de Angola*, People's Air Force of Angola

FAPLA – *Forças Armadas Populares de Libertação de Angola*, People's Armed Forces for the Liberation of Angola, the MPLA's military wing, or army

FFAR – forward-firing air rockets

Fire Force – an airborne offensive force comprising combinations of gunships, offensive firepower, troopers, command and control, Bosboks, recce or Telstar, Pumas, insertion of stopper groups and troops—usually highly trained Parabats

Flossie – C-130 Hercules used as the air link between South Africa and South West Africa during the border war (slang)

FLOT – forward line of own troops, a very necessary requirement during close air support operations, to ensure safety of own forces

FNLA – *Frente Nacional para a Libertação de Angola*, National Front for the Liberation of Angola

FRELIMO – *Frente de Libertação de Moçambique*, Liberation Front of Mozambique

FTS – Flying Training School

G – gravity. Under normal circumstances everything on earth is affected by the pull of gravity, called 1G. In tight turns or loops, centrifugal force effectively increases the pull of gravity. A G meter in the cockpit registers this increase. Readings of –2 to +7G are the usual range experienced during a typical fighter sortie. At =7G, the body's blood effectively becomes seven times heavier than normal and hastens the onset of blackout as blood drains towards the pilot's feet. At –G readings blood is forced to the head, sometimes resulting in 'red-out' when the capillary blood vessels in the eyes burst from the increased pressure

Gatup – a high-G manoeuvre developed by 1 Squadron pilots which affords maximum safety for an aircraft in a hostile environment. A 4G pull-up is followed by a 120–130° banked turn as the pilot pulls the sight onto the target. Immediately thereafter, he fires a laser shot to accurately measure range to the target. The pilot then pulls the nose skyward. The laser input allows the computer to predict an automatic release of the bombs during the pull-up. After bomb release, the pilot reapplies G, overbanks and pulls the aircraft's nose down toward the ground. The escape from the target area is flown at low level. When this manoeuvre is performed at night it is termed *Nagup*

GCA – ground-controlled approach, radar talk-down used to guide pilots to a safe landing in bad weather or at night

GCI – ground-controlled interception

GOC SWA – General Officer Commanding South West Africa

GP – general purpose

Grad-P – single-shot 122mm Soviet rocket launcher, mounted on a tripod and able to fire a 46kg rocket with an 18.3kg warhead a maximum distance of 11,000m. Much used by SWAPO for their stand-off bombardments

G-suit – the inflatable garment zipped around abdomen and legs that inhibits blood flow to the pilot's feet as aircraft G-loading is increased

guns free – the state prevailing when all guns are allowed to fire at designated targets as and when they are ready; only ordered when no own forces' aircraft are in the area

guns tight – the order given to cease own forces' artillery firing when own forces' aircraft are operating over a battlefield

HAA – helicopter administration area, *see* HAG

HAG – *helikopter administrasie gebied*, Afrikaans for helicopter administration area (HAA); a designated area planned and secured by ground forces from where helicopters operated to expedite operations. Very often it was co-located with a forward headquarters where immediate tactical plans were coordinated. Fuel in drums or bladders was available to refuel the helicopters, with extra gunship ammunition available. The HAG could be stationary for two or three days depending on the area but longer than that was considered dangerous as SWAPO could be expected to locate the HAG in that time. On the border the Afrikaans HAG was always used, as the sound came more easily to the tongue.

HC – Honoris Crux, the highest decoration for military valour that could be awarded to members of the SADF/SAAF. There were three classes, namely HC Bronze, HC Silver and HC Gold

HE – high explosive

HF – high frequency (radio)

hopper – a high-frequency radio that has the facility for hopping from one frequency to another during broadcast, thus improving the security of messages and signals

HQ – headquarters

HUD – head-up display, the sighting system mounted in the front windscreen of a cockpit. Information displayed relieves the pilot of having to look inside the cockpit during critical manoeuvres

IAS – indicated air speed

IFR – in-flight refuelling/instrument flight rules, when flying in bad weather or at night

IMC – instrument meteorological conditions, used when it is mandatory to fly with sole reference to aircraft instrumentation

Impala – a single-engine, light jet ground-attack aircraft used very successfully throughout the bush war, by day and by night, and armed with 68mm rockets, bombs and 30mm cannon

interdiction – offensive mission flown with the aim of disrupting the enemy's logistical lines of communication

IP – initial point, a well-defined navigational position from where navigation or attack profiles can be commenced with accuracy

IRT – instrument rating test, an annual requirement for all pilots

JARIC – Joint Air Reconnaissance Intelligence Centre

JATS – Joint Air Training Scheme

JPT – jet pipe temperature

KIAS – knots indicated air speed

kill – during simulated ACM, missile launch or gun firing is expressed as a 'kill'

kts - knots

Kudu – a single-piston-engine, high-wing battlefield communication aircraft with capacity for six passengers (provided the temperature was not too high) or a limited quantity of freight

LABS – low-altitude bombing system. The system was originally designed to 'throw' tactical nuclear weapons in a toss-type manoeuvre. The launch aircraft pulls up from low level at high speeds and releases the bomb as the nose passes 45° above the horizon. The aircraft continues in a looping manoeuvre to escape the detonation, while the bomb flies nearly five miles before exploding. Never a very accurate method of delivery but sufficient for a nuclear blast

LIP – low intercept profile (later changed to UNCIP, *see* UNCIP)

LMG – light machine gun

LP – local population; a more common usage was PB, from the Afrikaans *plaaslike bevolking*

LZ – landing zone

maanskyn – moonlight, moonshine (Afrikaans)

Mach – as the speed of sound varies with temperature and altitude, Mach + number is used to refer to the aircraft's speed as a percentage of the speed of sound, e.g. Mach 1.0 = speed of sound and Mach 0.9 = 9/10ths of that speed (which also equates to 9nms per minute)

MAOT – mobile air operations team; the air force team usually comprised an OC (pilot), an operations officer, an intelligence officer, a radio operator and one or two clerks. The team plus their equipment could be airlifted into a tactical headquarters co-located with the army or police, or could move with the ground forces in mine-protected vehicles as an integral part of the command headquarters. The OC of the team was often called 'the MAOT'

Mayday – international distress call

medevac – medical evacuation; differs from casevac as the patient is already under medical supervision and being transported to a more suitable medical centre

MF – medium frequency (radio)

MHz – megahertz, to denote frequency band

MiG – Mikoyan-Gurevich, the Soviet-designed family of jet fighters. The Angolan Air Force was equipped with the delta-winged MiG-21 and later the swing-wing MiG-23 variety

Military Region – for military purposes the border areas inside South West Africa immediately adjacent to the Angolan border were divided into the Kaokoland, Sector 10 Owamboland, Sector 20 Kavango and Sector 70 Caprivi Strip. The Angolans, however, divided their country into Military Regions. The 5th Military Region faced Kaokoland and Sector 10, while the 6th Military Region faced Kavango and Caprivi

Mirage – French-built Dassault, the family of supersonic fighters used by the SAAF

MPLA – *Movimento Popular de Libertação de Angola*, Popular Movement for the Liberation of Angola

MRG – master reference gyro, the main gyro which controls all the flying instruments in a Buccaneer. Failure of the 'master' can, under certain circumstances, cause the crew instant dyspepsia, hysteria and can be accompanied by uncontrollable tears

MRU – mobile radar unit

Nagup – the night equivalent of *Gatup* (*see Gatup*)

NATO – North Atlantic Treaty Organization

NDB – non-directional beacon; navigational aid which transmits a signal in all directions except immediately overhead. Pilots using their ADF instrument can lock on to the NDB to receive directional information from the beacon

OAU – Organization of African Unity

OC – officer commanding

OC WAC – Officer Commanding Western Air Command

OCU – operational conversion unit

Ops Co – operations co-ordinator

ops normal – a radio transmission made at regular intervals, usually 20 minutes, allowing command-post staff to monitor the progress of low-level missions

Parabat – Parachute Battalion soldier, qualified to wear the famous red beret

PI – photographic interpreter

PLAN – People's Liberation Army of Namibia, SWAPO's military wing

PNR – point of no return

pongo – an infantryman, a 'brown job' (SADF and British Army slang)

PR – photographic reconnaissance

Puma – a twin-engine transport helicopter that carried a crew of three and 16 lightly armed or 12 fully armed troops

PUP – pull-up point

RAF – Royal Air Force

RAMS – radio-activated marker system

Recce – Reconnaissance Commando (Special Forces)

recce – reconnaissance, as in ground recce, an airborne visual recce, a photographic recce or an EW (electronic) recce of a point or area

RhAF – Rhodesian Air Force

RP – rocket projectile

RPG – rocket-propelled grenade

RPG-7 – rocket-propelled grenade, an anti-tank, tube-launched grenade of Soviet origin with a maximum effective range of 500m and an explosive warhead weighing 2.4kg. It is robust, 'soldier-proof', easy to use and much favoured by insurgents worldwide

RPV – remotely piloted vehicle/aircraft

RSA – Republic of South Africa

RV – rendezvous, the chosen point usually a grid reference on a map, an easily recognizable ground feature or a bearing and distance from a navigational facility

RWR/RWS – radar warning receiver/system

SAAC – South African Aviation Corps

SAAF – South African Air Force

SADF – South African Defence Force

SADF – South African Defence Force (pre-1994)

SAM – surface-to-air missile, a missile, guided by infrared or radar, fired from a launcher on the ground at an airborne target. By the end of the war the Angolans had an array of missiles which included SA-2 fixed site, SA-3 fixed site, SA-6 mobile, tracked, SA-7 shoulder-launched*, SA-8 mobile, wheeled, SA-9 mobile, wheeled, SA-13 mobile, tracked, SA-14 shoulder-launched, SA-16 shoulder-launched. (*SWAPO used only the SA-7 but FAPLA was equipped with the entire range)

SAMS – South African Medical Services

SANDF – South African National Defence Force (post 1994)

SAP – South African Police

SAR – search and rescue

SATCO – Senior Air Traffic Control Officer

scramble – traditional term used when fighter aircraft are ordered to take off immediately

shona – a shallow pan or an open area in the bush that fills with rain during the rainy season and is invariably dry during the winter months. Also *chana* in Angola

SOP – standard operating procedure, common parlance for anything that is a standard, recognized drill

SSO Ops – Senior Staff Officer Operations

SWA – South West Africa, now Namibia

SWAPO – South West African People's Organization

SWAPOL – South West African Police

SWATF – South West African Territorial Force; both the SADF and SWATF were commanded by GOC SWA

tac HQ – a tactical headquarters instituted for the running of an operation close to the combat zone, commanded by a subordinate commander with guidelines and limitations delegated by a sector headquarters

Tacan – tactical air navigation facility

tail-dragger – any propeller-driven aircraft that has two main wheels and a third under the tail. This aircraft requires different techniques when approaching and taking off from those used by the more usual tricycle-configured aircraft

Telstar – an aircraft flown at medium altitude to relay VHF messages from aircraft on low-flying operational missions

TF – task force

tiffie – a mechanic, from the word 'artificer' (military slang)

TOD – top of descent

top cover – aerial cover; aircraft were considered prestige targets by the SWAPO insurgents. Aircraft are at their most vulnerable when taking off or landing in the vicinity of airfields. At Ondangwa, therefore, an Alouette gunship was airborne for all movements of fixed-wing transport aircraft. The gunship carried out a wide left-hand orbit of the airfield to counter any attempt by guerrillas to fire at the transport aircraft. The concept was also used in combat areas to cover own ground troops or to make-safe landing zones for troop-carrying helicopters in the bush

TOT – time on target

transonic zone – the speed band where the airflow over the aircraft alters from subsonic to supersonic flow, usually between Mach 0.9 to 1.1. As the aircraft transits through this zone, changes to the centre of pressure can affect stability

Typhoon – SWAPO's elite group of highly trained troops whose specific task was the deep infiltration of South West Africa. Although highly esteemed by SWAPO, they did not achieve any more notable successes than the ordinary cadres; also referred to as Vulcan or Volcano troops

UDF – Union Defence Force (pre-1957)

UNCIP – unconventional interception profile

Unimog – a 2.5-litre 4x4 Mercedes Benz transport vehicle that bore the brunt of bush operations until SWAPO mine-laying hastened the introduction of mine-protected vehicles

UNITA – *União Nacional para a Independência Total de Angola*, National Union for the Total Independence of Angola

UNTAG – United Nations Transitional Agreement Group

USSR – Union of Soviet Socialist Republics

ZANLA – Zimbabwe African National Liberation Army, ZANU's military wing

ZANU – Zimbabwe African National Union

ZAPU – Zimbabwe African People's Union

ZIPRA – Zimbabwe People's Revolutionary Army, ZAPU's military wing

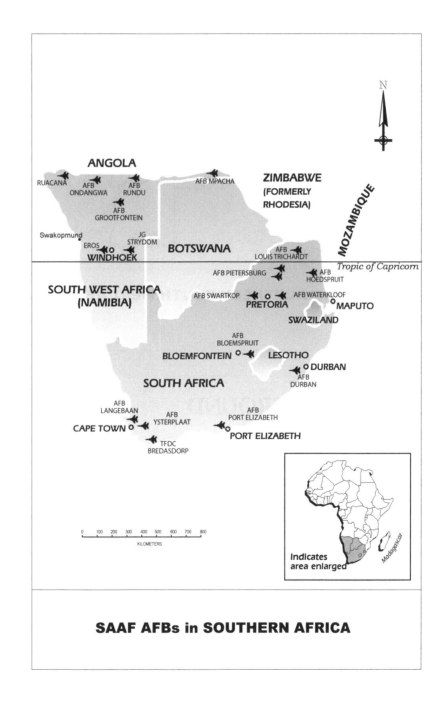

SAAF AFBs in SOUTHERN AFRICA

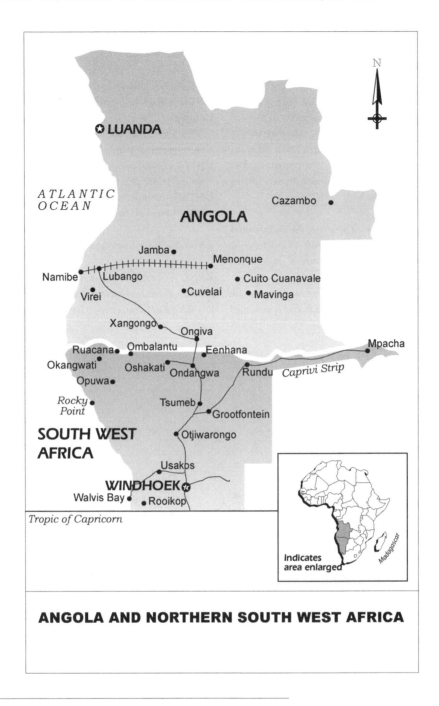

ANGOLA AND NORTHERN SOUTH WEST AFRICA

A BRIEF HISTORICAL BACKGROUND

At the end of 1987 and the beginning of 1988 the first conventional tank battle to be fought in Africa since the Second World War and the only one of its kind ever to take place in sub-Saharan Africa was fought over a large expanse of the dense savannah woodland of southern Angola. This was the Battle of Cuito Cuanavale, a series of operations that marked the climax to what has since come to be known as the South African Border War and, moreover, the concluding military chapter of the African Liberation Struggle.

The Battle of Cuito Cuanavale and the slow culmination of events that led up to it, although not specifically related to the South West African war of independence upon which the Border War was largely premised, was a clash of titans that had always

been promised once the tide of black liberation – the *swart gevaar*, or 'black threat' – finally reached the borders of South Africa itself. Cuito Cuanavale was more directly a factor of the Angolan civil war, with South Africa acting ostensibly in support of a faction within that conflict, although with the unmistakable strategic objective of securing the border region of South West Africa through this proxy support.

The African liberation period began in the post-Second World War period with the rise of African nationalism, continent-wide, and a concurrent decline of the European appetite for foreign territorial domination. The process, notwithstanding a certain inherent violence, flared into war in key regions where settler

The South West African border with Angola as depicted in this old German map.

minorities sought to resist the inevitable. The most notable of these were Algeria, Kenya, Mozambique, Angola and Rhodesia. The process continued throughout the 1960s, 1970s and 1980s, culminating only in 1994 with the eventual handover of power in Pretoria to a black government voted into office by an authentic majority.

South Africa has always been different from any other territory on the continent of Africa and certainly in sub-Saharan Africa. Militarily and economically, the country hardly occupies the same league as any other nation in the region. With the possible exception of white Rhodesia, the South African Defence Force has been, and remains, unequalled on a per-capita basis by any indigenous military organization anywhere else on the continent.

How and why did South Africa emerge as such a regional superpower? The answer to this is complex and not without a strong hint of the composite race ideology that has been, and perhaps remains, so much a factor in the existence of South Africa as a country. The territory was settled early, with Dutch settlers making landfall in the mid-17th century, and was liberated late. Thus the territory enjoyed a little over 300 years of Europeanization which, whatever might be the current liberation ideology, allowed for the deep entrenchment of western-style civilization and the generation of stable institutions of government over a much longer period than say Kenya or indeed Southern Rhodesia. The latter was removed from the map of Africa in 1980 after a mere 90 years of modern existence.

South Africa has also enjoyed almost unprecedented natural endowments in the form of gold and diamonds which were discovered in the latter half of the 19th century and which at the time were recognized as being the most concentrated deposits in the world. This, needless to say, transformed what had hitherto been a rather lowly and unimportant colonial backwater to arguably the most important theatre of capital adventure and warfare in the entire British Empire. An astonishing amount of wealth began to circulate within the various economies of South Africa, with a great deal more than this finding its way back to various European capital markets, London being perhaps the most important.

No less important were the political ramifications of this transformation. The Cape had been settled by Dutch East India Company men for the purpose of supplying passing vessels en route to the Indies. These had been followed later by waves of Huguenot religious exiles who brought with them the higher

A Buccaneer going down Brandberg in South West Africa.

cultural sensibilities of their French ancestry. In combination with the Dutch, they evolved a fusion culture that, in the isolation of such an out-of-the-way settlement, developed language, traditions and peculiarities very different from their metropolitan cousins and certainly unlike anything else underway at that time in sub-Saharan Africa. The Portuguese settled the region earlier but tended to apply a lacklustre style of colonialism that saw the evolution of sea ports such as Luanda and Lourenço Marques (Maputo) but little else. The Portuguese always regretted the fact that they failed to occupy the Cape in time to thwart the arrival of other European powers.

Although highly cultured at their core, the Afrikaner nation, as this new sub-culture identified itself, also comprised a highly parochial outer fringe made up of frontier farmers and herdsmen who spread out over several generations to occupy a significant swath of territory in the hinterland of the Cape. A certain independence of mind also developed among these frontier families who, for much of their early existence, suffered no territorial constraint and certainly had to bear very little interference from any central authority. They developed a highly individualistic, and somewhat backward-looking, cultural identity that had about it a strong strain of ethnocentrism and manifest destiny.

It therefore goes without saying that in the aftermath of the Napoleonic Wars when the British inherited the bulk of East Indian trade interests and consequently took over the administration of the Cape for much the same reasons as the Dutch had, these far-flung Afrikaner communities of the sub-continent would suddenly feel deeply impinged-upon and wholly unwilling to submit to the far more intrusive style of territorial administration

A Buccaneer streaks through Soussesvlei, South West Africa.

Desert dust: the hazards of air-mobile warfare in South West Africa.

that the British tended to introduce.

From that point on a deep antipathy was born between the two races, felt most acutely by the Afrikaner, for it was their Abrahamic view of themselves as a gifted race that was being compromised and their long-cherished liberties that were being curtailed. In the early 1800s the more radical among the Afrikaner leadership began to ponder an exodus across the Orange River, then the farthest limit of organized European settlement, and north into the great unknown interior in order that they might found a new nation apart from the British and beyond any trace of outside interference. Thus, during the 1830s and 1840s, one of the most dramatic human migrations ever recorded played out as the *volk*, the people, decamped from the Cape in large numbers and struck north into the great unknown.

From this great defining event of the Afrikaner nation emerged two independent republics, the Orange Free State and the Transvaal. This rendered the sub-continent south of the Limpopo River a patchwork of colonies and half-republics that were locked in an extremely unhappy marriage of proximity which, once again, tended to favour the more progressive and modernist British. This fact was driven home most cruelly when the first diamonds began to be unearthed in the dry soil of Griqualand West. A swath of country of little natural appeal, long ignored by both the British of the Cape and the Boer of the Orange Free State, and nominally falling under Orange Free State territorial claim, almost overnight

became of vital strategic importance to both, and in the classic style of 'Britannia waives the rules' was arbitrarily delineated to the Cape whose economy it thereafter magnificently transformed.

The same was true for gold which was discovered in the Transvaal in enormous quantities and which in 1886 set in motion a gold rush that was to change the political and social landscape of the republic in ways that dismayed the isolationist Boer. Neither joy nor relief was brought to the Transvaal by this great discovery; it instead flooded the key economic centres of the republic with a deluge of fortune seekers from all over the known world in a classic gold rush scenario, threatening to sink the heavy republican boat now swilling to the gunwales with British capital and influence. For how could it have been otherwise? Men like Cecil Rhodes, Alfred Beit and many others possessed a degree of financial acumen that was almost entirely absent among the bedrock of the Afrikaners. These foreigners, *uitlanders*, amassed huge fortunes in gold and diamonds, gaining phenomenal influence as they did, influence that they tended to direct not toward the interests of the republic but toward greater British control of the region.

From this the inevitability of war grew and, indeed, hostilities erupted on 11 October 1899 in what has come to be known as the Second Anglo–Boer War. The first war had taken place toward the end of 1880 and had little military, but massive political, significance. Although the Boers were inevitably defeated, the military lore of the Anglo–Boer War spins a tale of such courage, commitment, endurance and Christian-like fortitude on the part of the conquered that, and not only in their own eyes, the Boer without doubt won the moral war.

From this defining experience, however, the chastened Afrikaner nation threw up international statesmen of the calibre of Louis Botha and Jan Smuts. For newcomers to South African history, both these men had been key guerrilla leaders during the closing phases of the Anglo–Boer War, each in his own theatre fighting the British with extraordinary creativity and absolute commitment – thereafter transmogrifying into *British* statesmen at the helm of an unquiet *British* crown dominion.

It was this curious fact that complicated South African involvement in the First World War. Upon the signing of a peace agreement, the British had drawn the curtain on the Anglo–Boer War, accepting the investiture of the Union of South Africa into the British imperial family – thereafter moving on to matters of European instability – with little thought given to how the defeated grassroots Afrikaans-speakers of South Africa might view the evaporation of their republics and their implied fealty to the hated institution of the British Crown. Botha and Smuts effectively led this new British overseas territory, serving as British proxies. This naturally enraged many among their erstwhile followers who saw in this a betrayal of the blood of their comrades and of their Afrikaner identity.

Thus, when the task was given to Prime Minister Botha to deal with an entrenched enemy force in the adjacent German territory of South West Africa, many on the ground felt that it was not the Germans who were the natural enemies of South

Africa but the British. A brief and somewhat quixotic rebellion occurred among front-line South African units that, although it did not particularly threaten South Africa as a crown dominion, did complicate military preparations for the occupation of South West Africa, giving hope to some that with German support the British could be overthrown and the republics re-instituted.

In the end the disturbance was put down and a brilliant campaign was fought by the armed forces of South Africa to assume the territory of South West Africa for the Allies and to neutralize the local German garrison force. This was an important moment in the history of South Africa, in particular with regards to how matters would evolve later in the century, for after the war the territory was made over to South Africa as a League of Nations mandate, effectively handing it over to South Africa as something more than a colony but somewhat less than a fifth province. At a later point, and in a more enlightened global political environment, pressure would be brought to bear against South Africa to relinquish control of the territory which, under the influence of a more nationalistic mind set, she refused to do.

This then sets the stage for the war that would ignite some 50 years later as indigenous Namibians sought to reclaim control of the territory through popular revolution. This state of affairs, of course, was not unique to South Africa. The power of European empire had been deeply compromised by the events of the First World War and even more so by the Second. The Atlantic Charter, a policy document signed by both Franklin D. Roosevelt and Winston Churchill, sought to define the character of a post-war globe, pivotal to which would be the right to self-determination of all the peoples of the world. The first substantive territory to respond to this was India which was granted independence in 1948, followed by a raft of British, French and other sundry European overseas territories across the colonial spectrum.

In Africa the colonies of pure economic interest – those, for example, that hosted limited independent European settlement other than expatriate economic or administrative staff – were handed over relatively painlessly. Others, however, such as Kenya

and Algeria and, farther south, Rhodesia, Mozambique and Angola, all of which had been extensively settled by European populations that derived their existence from a local economy, held on for some sort of guarantee of political predominance over the black majority, or parity at the very least, eventually becoming the focus of revolutionary wars that now define much of the mythology of the black liberation struggle.

Four bitter, divisive and bloody liberation wars were fought in the region before the final focus fell on South Africa itself in the great and global anti-apartheid movement of the 1980s. These were the Mozambican and Angolan wars fought concurrently by Portugal to suppress local liberation movements, the Rhodesian war which, although of a somewhat different character, was defined by the same basic principles, and the war for the liberation of South West Africa which is partly the focus of this narrative.

It is not possible, however, to examine one without at least making reference to each of the others, for each in many ways was interlinked, and as each territory fell in sequence, the general movement toward liberation was strengthened, quite as the rather plaintive defence of the line by minority European regimes was weakened.

Of importance also is the fact that the war in South West Africa differed in certain key areas from any other that had been fought hitherto. South Africa was, and remains, a regional superpower, with characteristics both militarily and economically that have more in common with the developed world than the developing world. To even a casual visitor to South Africa this is quite evident, with a national freeway system and transport infrastructure, as just one example, that is by world standards impressive and by African standards miraculous.

Similarly, the national civic structure, the industrial infrastructure and the institutions of government, law enforcement and defence in South Africa hardly bear comparison with any other nation-state in the region. It stands to reason, therefore, that wherever South Africa should choose to stand and fight there would be a fight indeed.

CHAPTER ONE:
BACKGROUND TO THE SAAF

And so it was, but here we are specifically concerned with the South African Air Force, and its role in the South African Border War that was fought between 1966 and 1989. The SAAF as an institution has enjoyed an august reputation and a history concurrent with all the major contributing nations of the world. The Wright Brothers, of course, achieved the first powered flight in a heavier-than-air machine but quickly thereafter others began to experiment with and improve upon the principle. The first aircraft constructed in South Africa was that imported and assembled by civil engineer

and South African aviation pioneer John Weston in Brandfort in 1907, although this particular machine did not achieve flight until it was completed in France three years later. The first powered aircraft to actually take to the air in South Africa was a Voisin single-sea-engine-powered pusher biplane belonging to a visiting French aviator, M. Albert Kimmerling, who demonstrated his craft briefly at the Nahoon Racecourse in East London. It was Weston, however, in 1911, who recorded what has since been accepted as the first confirmed sustained powered flight in South

A camouflaged SAAF DC-3 Dakota.

Impala flypast at Mpacha.

Africa. Weston thereafter established the John Weston Aviation Company and in the same year – 1911 – the Aeronautical Society of South Africa.

With the formation of the Union of South Africa in 1910, the first minister of defence, General Jan Smuts, set about moulding a unified military from the at times antagonistic remnants of the Anglo–Boer War. The Defence Act of 1912 established a Union Defence Force, command of which was given to General Christiaan Frederick Beyers who later persuaded Jan Smuts to consider the introduction of an air wing to the fledgling South African military formation. Contact was made with a certain Cecil Compton Paterson, another local aviation pioneer, who began training the first draft of ten would-be aviators at his flying school located just outside Kimberley, forming the nucleus of the South African Aviation Corps (SAAC), a branch of the Active Citizen Force (ACF).

Within a few years the world was at war and the value of aircraft in battle was put to the test. South African pilots were absorbed into the Royal Flying Corps, as were aviators from across the imperial spectrum, including from the Rhodesias.[1] In South West Africa the SAAC flew in support of South African forces under the direct command of generals Botha and Smuts, flying in a reconnaissance role for the most part, achieving little as an offensive tool, with bombing sorties tending to be highly experimental and rarely effective. The same was largely true for the Germans.

Notwithstanding constrained post-war economics, meanwhile, 1 February 1920 saw the appointment of South Africa's first Director of Air Services and the establishment of the South African Air Force. The imperial government allocated 100 sundry aircraft from its extensive war stocks, as it did for each of the dominion air forces, complete with a full complement of spares and equipment. At a later point, a further 13 aircraft were obtained from various other sources which brought the total up to 113. An aerodrome was established at Zwartkop, now Air Force Base (AFB) Swartkop, situated south of Pretoria and not far from the suburb of Waterkloof where one of the main South African air force bases is located.

Nearby too was the aircraft and artillery depot where, despite acute Depression-era fiscal difficulties, the early foundations of South Africa aeronautical industry were born. Here the general repair and maintenance of SAAF aircraft evolved into more specific aircraft modification and adaption, and then full assembly with the grant of a licence to locally build the Westland Wapiti, a British two-seat general-purpose military single-engine biplane, with the first locally-built variant taking to the air on 4 April 1931.

At the same time the SAAF itself grew at a steady pace with the establishment of three new squadrons, bringing the total to seven, and the construction of new stations and bases at Waterkloof, Bloemfontein, Durban and Youngsfield. A central flying school was also established with satellite training centres located in each of the provinces.

Notwithstanding all this, South Africa was caught somewhat on the back foot by the outbreak of the Second World War. The country did, however, now have excellent training and base facilities which, alongside the natural attributes of climate and landscape, made South Africa a fairly obvious choice to be part of the proposed Empire Air Training Scheme. This was a series of empire-wide agreements whereby the key dominions would host and help train RAF airmen. Training in the skies over England itself while the Battle of Britain was on was hardly feasible and the RAF needed to rapidly build up the necessary manpower resources that would be needed once the brave few holding back the Luftwaffe over the English Channel had done their work.

It is interesting to note that a number of empire pilots were present among 'the few' during that great and iconic air battle of the Second World War, among them Rhodesians and South Africans, 25 of the latter, with some aces among them. A 1941 news item from United Press made this remark: "The Royal Air Force disclosed today the identities of its ten leading aces. One is a former financial clerk in a newspaper office; another, a former South African sailor. One has artificial legs; one is only 22 years

Mirage IIIR2Z being towed from the revetments at AFB Hoedspruit.

the meanwhile, also took part in the Berlin Airlift that shuttled vital supplies to cut-off West Berlin during the Soviet blockade of the city in 1948.

It was in that year too that the SAAF began to shed a little of its imperial complexion and move more toward an entity of specific South African identity. This came about as a consequence of the return to power of the Afrikaans-speaking majority in the landmark election of 1948, a crossroads for South Africa in many ways, as it was more or less at this moment that the key race statutes began to be assembled that would define South Africa in the latter part of the century as a polarized and steeply xenophobic nation.

old; one shot down six German planes in six hours." The South African sailor was Adolph Gysbert Malan, the celebrated fighter pilot who led 74 Squadron RAF through the Battle of Britain, surviving the war with a record of 27 confirmed kills and three probables.

South Africa's contribution to the EATS was a parallel agreement with the acronym JATS, or Joint Air Training Scheme, which provided for 38 local air schools to train SAAF, RAF and other Allied air- and groundcrews for service overseas. The aircraft necessary to undertake this were provided by the British Air Ministry. By the end of 1941, SAAF personnel levels had jumped to some 34,000, 956 of whom were pilots. By the time JATS was wound down toward the end of the war, 33,347 aircrew, including 12,221 SAAF members, had passed through the system. These men were spread across the global theatre of war, joining airmen from across the imperial spectrum, serving in East Africa, North Africa, Asia and Europe, and flying a total of 82,401 missions for the loss of 2,227 SAAF servicemen.

In the aftermath of the war the bulk of South African troops and airmen serving overseas was demobilized and both the Union Defence Force and the SAAF returned to peacetime status. The SAAF was reduced in size to its essential Permanent Force (regular) component, supported by additional active Citizens Force (territorial) units. Development cooperation with Britain continued in the afterglow of victory with the arrival in the territory of a small flight of Gloster Meteor III jet fighters, sent out on trials and flown by the SAAF for two years before being returned to the UK. The arrival was also recorded of the first helicopter to be flown in South Africa, a Sikorsky 5-51 purchased from the USA, one of three that would eventually be absorbed into service in the country. South African Air Force aircrews, in

As many other restive colonies and emerging nation states were likewise doing, South Africa at that time began to distance itself from British imperial interests, quite as the Empire itself was beginning to show signs of weakening in key areas of the world, Africa not least of these. This weaning of a nascent republic away from British support also coincided with a significant hardening of political attitudes within the country, in particular in the matter of race policy and race delineation, which in turn laid the foundations of apartheid, further isolating South Africa and setting the tone for the growth of liberation movements and the anti-apartheid struggle of the 1970s and 1980s.

Practically, this involved the standing down of the current Active Citizen Force, the territorial quotient of the UDF, for fear that it tended to identify more closely with the imperial parentage of the South African armed forces and, in particular, the SAAF for the fact that as a strata of the armed services it was the airmen – educated and liberal for the most part – who tended to be affected most by British airs and graces. Contracts were not renewed and budgets constrained in an effort to weed out any, or as many as possible, of those who were not sympathetic to South African independence or the emerging National Party agenda.

The SAAF pulled against this somewhat by adopting air force blues and affecting a more British type of air force culture, epitomized by the RAF squadron traditions, which those within it would have recognized and identified with instantly, but which those without would have seen as being more than a little elitist and exclusive. Despite this, in November 1950, the SAAF adopted the Springbok motif for the centre of the roundel, giving the SAAF an authentic and individual identity. Also that year the de Havilland

The South African contingent at Dassault Aviation, France, 1974.

Mirage F1AZ armed with eight 460kg bombs.

domestic Cheetah C aircraft would be developed, evolving, as we will hear later, into a virtual modern fifth-generation fighter.

South Africa, along with Israel, was one of the first nations, other than France itself, to see the potential of the Mirage III, acquiring 16 Mirage IIICZ interceptors between 1962 and 1964 (the Z indicated aircraft specifically supplied to South Africa). These were followed by three Mirage IIIBZ two-seaters and four Mirage II-IRZ reconnaissance fighters. The first Mirage fighter squadron was 2 Squadron, the famous Flying Cheetahs, based at AFB Waterkloof and calling upon an illustrious pedigree established during several years of adrenaline-fuelled service in Korea.

These aircraft proved to be so satisfactory that a second order for 17 Mirage IIIEZs was issued even before the complete complement of aircraft previously ordered had arrived in the country. These aircraft were developed and manufactured for the fighter-bomber role with improved avionics, being incorporated first into SAAF 2 Squadron but later forming the core of the newly-activated SAAF 3 Squadron, also based at AFB Waterkloof. In addition, three Mirage IIIDZ trainers and eleven Mirage IIIDZ2s were acquired along with four additional Mirage IIIR2Z reconnaissance-fighters.

As a postscript to this short introductory biography of the Mirage III in service in South Africa, the aircraft did prove to be something of a disappointment once the air war over Angola got underway.

Despite being recognized as a superb fighter, the Mirage III lacked the range to make it effective over the long distances involved in combat, ground-strike and interdiction missions deep into Angola which became the norm from the mid-1980s. Where it did come into its own, however, was in photo-reconnaissance missions flown over heavily defended targets, which utilized the Mirage IIIRZ and R2Z, as work of this nature was considered too dangerous for the more vulnerable Canberra light bombers traditionally earmarked for this kind of work.

The Blackburn Buccaneer fleet would also prove to be a vital

DH100 Vampire, the SAAF's first jet fighter, was brought into service, replacing the Second World War-era Spitfires that then began to be phased out, along with the venerable Venturas and Sunderlands that until that point had been the bedrock of the force. In 1956, 34 North American Aviation CL-13B Mk VI Sabres found their way into service, followed in the 1960s by the acquisition of a fleet of Mirage IIIs, English Electric Canberra light bombers, Blackburn Buccaneer and Lockheed Hercules C-130 aircraft.

The Sabres were never used in any significant way during the Border War (they had given magnificent service in Korea) and were phased out before hostilities reached a level requiring air intervention, but the Mirage IIIs were a success story, beginning something of a love affair that the SAAF would have with various Dassault Aviation Mirage marks, the Mirage IIIs being of particular interest because it was upon this aircraft that the

The Blackburn Buccaneer.

A Buccaneer with an H2 bomb on the inner pylon and an EW pod on the outer pylon under the port wing. The H2 communications pod is under the starboard wing.

Dick Lord, seen here after his first solo in an F-86 Sabre.

component of the SAAF offensive capacity during the long Border War, with its low-level strike facility proving invaluable in hundreds of operations aimed at known target positions and general interdiction throughout the late 1970s and 1980s. It was able to carry eight 1,000lb bombs, among other armaments, and as senior SAAF commander and chronicler Brigadier-General Dick Lord observed: "The Buccaneer was perhaps the best aircraft in the SAAF arsenal in terms of an African war. It could fly fast and low over great distances while carrying everything plus the kitchen sink." The Buccaneer initially delivered its payload from a dive-bombing profile but altered this to the toss-bomb technique once enemy ground defences – missiles and radar deployment and usage – began to improve. South Africa was in fact the only nation other than Britain to operate Buccaneers.

The first aircraft arrived in South Africa as a consequence of the Simon's Town Agreement, a naval cooperation accord between Britain and South Africa signed on 30 June 1955. Under the terms of agreement South Africa would receive weapons for the defence of the vital shipping lanes around the Cape in exchange for British rights to the use of Simon's Town naval base near Cape Town.

The Buccaneer was modified prior to delivery to suit local geographic and climatic demands, producing the S. Mk 50, an improvement on the standard S2, that included a strengthened undercarriage and higher capacity wheel-braking system with manually folded wings. In-flight refuelling was also considered a prerequisite, as well as longer-range 430-gallon underwing tanks. In addition, engineering staff at Blackburn fitted an assisted take-off mechanism that comprised two retractable Bristol-Siddeley BS605 rocket engines which gave 30s of additional thrust during take-off and which were located at the rear of the aircraft toward the back of the engine nacelle. South Africa was the only operator of the S. Mk 50, a total of 16 being ordered in January 1963. The aircraft were flown by 24 Squadron until its disbanding in 1991 soon after the end of the war in South West Africa.

The Buccaneers were often flown in formation with another workhorse of offensive and photo-reconnaissance operations throughout the air war in South West Africa and Angola: the English Electric Canberra. Flown by the SAAF's 12 Squadron, the Canberra was an elegant, streamlined and highly functional jet-powered light bomber. The general service history of this aircraft is impressive, being used in the Vietnam War, the Falklands War, the Indo-Pakistani wars as well as a number of African conflicts, most notably the South African air war over Angola, the Rhodesian civil war where it was a stalwart in external raids over Mozambique and Zambia, and in the Ethiopian Air Force in a number of regional flare-ups.

An Impala firing a full salvo of rockets.

A tiffie checks that a Matra missile is secure.

Super Frelons.

Two of the many variants of the Canberra were operated by the SAAF: the B (1).12 and the T.4. The first of the B (1).12s was acquired in 1963, with six ultimately being introduced into service along with three trainers, all flown by 12 Squadron. In 1980 a second-hand bomber-variant nose cone was acquired from Rhodesia which allowed one of the T.4s to be converted to a bomber role which coincided with the gradual internationalization of the air war and the need for as many practical air assets as possible.

The Canberra fleet saw consistent service throughout the air war, being used primarily as low-level bombers, notwithstanding a recognized high-altitude facility, with a capacity to deliver up to 300 alpha bombs from a deep bomb bay that was also configured to deploy both 250kg and the ubiquitous 1,000lb general-purpose bombs.

Canberras were a key component in two of the most effective airstrikes of the war. During the 1983 Operation *Askari*, Canberras combined with Impalas to destroy Angolan defences at Cuvelai which allowed SADF ground forces to capture the town at a significantly reduced human and material cost. Later, a combined Canberra–Buccaneer formation, the latter armed with AS-30 missiles, neutralized strong enemy fortifications at Cangamba in southern Angola which allowed UNITA to capture the town after nine days of heavy but inconclusive fighting.

The bomber version or the Canberra utilized a glass nose to enable the navigator–bomb-aimer to aim the bombs through a gyroscopically-stabilized gun sight, while the pilot(s) were positioned under an offset tear-drop canopy. In its photo-reconnaissance role a bomber-variant camera – usually a Zeiss F-96, but occasionally an Omega-6 – was contained in a conformal gun pack canoe supplied with the original British airframes. As many as five, but usually three Zeiss cameras would be arranged in a fan configuration, with the 6-inch Omega allowing a wider field for PI orientation. There would also be a 36-inch Zeiss F-96 arranged as a vertical pinpoint camera, although the 48-inch lens was used infrequently thanks to the difficulty of keeping points of interest within the banana-slide aiming device used to manage acceptable tracking.

A circular rear camera hatch/bay was also typically used to mount the prime vertical F-96. This camera was employed during low-level strike missions for BDA photography by mounting an optical mirror looking at 45 degrees aft/down. This recorded sequentially where the alpha bombs were about to or had just struck. This simple idea saved a considerable amount of time and avoided the necessity of sending a second aircraft back later to review the results of any operation.

The Buccaneer–Canberra combination was the workhorse of the SAAF air war, but arguably the jewel in the crown of SAAF fighter capacity throughout the period was the Mirage F1 fleet flown by SAAF 1 and 3 squadrons and which saw considerable and consistent action over Angola.

The Mirage F1 was developed as an air-superiority fighter, primarily to succeed the highly successful Mirage III mark, to which the SAAF was already committed and which had been in service internationally since the early 1960s. The FI was a private venture underwritten by Dassault in order to make available a cheaper multi-role aircraft, offering the best operational efficiency and the widest flexibility during a period of rapid technological development.

The F1 offered a number features attractive to the South African defence establishment in view of evolving operational conditions confronted by the SAAF. Chief among these was the ability of the aircraft to take off and land on short, rough airstrips, thanks to the twin pulled wheel on the main gear together with medium-pressure tyres and the aircraft's comparatively low landing speed. An additional advantage was the fact that ground-handling equipment was fully air transportable, combined with a self-starting system and a general operational turnaround time of about 15 minutes between complimentary or identical missions – the latter utilizing a pressure-refuelling time of about six minutes – all of which suited conditions in northern South West Africa where the aircraft would be operational for extended periods. Moreover, the SDAP testing unit allowed for automatic trouble-

Cameras housed in the nose of the Mirage III reconnaissance aircraft.
Photo SAAF Museum

part of which urged member nations to respect a voluntary arms embargo against South Africa. This was largely ignored and so was consequently bolstered in July 1970 by Resolution 283 which, although falling short of a mandatory arms embargo, again urged member nations to take all and any action possible to give effect to the resolution's measures.

The F1 purchase thereafter went ahead in some haste in an effort to beat the inevitable mandatory arms embargo that would eventually be contained in the measures of UN Security Council Resolution 418, adopted unanimously on 4 November 1977, and which effectively quarantined South Africa from regular external sources of arms and military equipment. The French, however, as had been the case with Rhodesia in 1965, showed themselves ever ready to thumb their noses at the rather high-minded British view of events in her erstwhile colonies and did what was possible under international scrutiny to fulfil what obligations were outstanding with South Africa.

South Africa ultimately acquired 16 Mirage F1-CZs and 32 Mirage F1-AZs. An interesting corollary of the undue haste of the programme was the question of pilots being available to man the Mirage III fleet, answered in 1972 by Operation *Sand*, the introduction of Rhodesian Air Force (RhAF) instructors, technicians and student pilots to various South African air bases for flight training. Rhodesian combat pilots, more at home in the venerable Hawker Hunters of the time, were also inducted temporality into 2 Squadron at AFB Waterkloof in order to man the fleet of Mirage IIIs. Part of Operation *Sand* was also a general strategic discussion on the idea of a NATO-style Southern African Treaty Organization that unfortunately evaporated with the collapse of Mozambique and Angola, removing two out of four potential partners.

Delivery of the F1s began under a blanket of secrecy in early April 1975 with the arrival by SAAF C-130 Hercules of two Mirage F1-CZs. Deliveries continued thus until October 1976, with the programme remaining top secret until the aircraft was revealed during a flypast at the Ysterplaat Air Show in 1975. It was not until April 1977 that the press were invited to the Kempton Park production line, although the entire programme remained officially classified until 1980.

So much for the front-line offensive capacity of the SAAF during the Border War. Warfare, however, be it on the ground or in the air, runs on the behind-the-scenes heavy lifting of logistics, supply and transport. The forward airbases located in South West Africa provided operational facilities for key operations and regular air force activity as it related to the ongoing war effort. Within South Africa itself there were 12 SAAF facilities scattered around the country: AFB Louis Trichardt, AFB Pietersburg, AFB Hoedspruit, AFB Swartkop, AFB Waterkloof, AFB Bloemspruit, AFB Durban, AFB Langebaan, AFB Ysterplaat, AFB Port Elizabeth and TFDC Bredasdorp. These provided homes to the various squadrons of the SAAF that periodically and, to a greater or lesser extent, were deployed on operations in the border region of South West Africa and in Angola. Four principal SAAF bases

shooting in the field while a GAMO alert unit enabled the Mirage F1 to be scrambled in less than two minutes. All this was to prove as close to ideal as was technically possible.

Thus, as South Africa began to consider replacements for the Mirage III, the F1 seemed an obvious choice. The F1 offered many improvements on the Mirage III in terms of speed, increased pursuit time and high mach, which was tripled, and twice the ground-mission range. Take-off length was some 30 per cent less than the III with a 25 per cent reduction in approach speed and a general increase in manoeuvrability. After many months of discussion and ongoing negotiation, it was announced in June 1971 that a technical cooperation agreement had been reached between Dassault and French aircraft-engine manufacturer Snecma on the one hand, and the South African Atlas Mirage programme on the other, for the licensed manufacture of the Mirage F1 and engine in South Africa, the intention being to locally produce up to 100 Mirage F1s.

However, international events, and the growing entrenchment of South African race policy in combination stole the moment. In 1964 hostile international diplomatic action against South Africa in condemnation of the deepening policy of apartheid resulted in United Nations Security Council Resolution 191, were used in South West Africa: AFB Ondangwa, AFB Rundu, AFB Mpacha and AFB Grootfontein, which was the largest and most comprehensively equipped.

A great deal of transit flying was undertaken between the home and forward bases, with helicopters and other aircraft being transported rather than flown, along with ground and maintenance equipment and associated personnel. Besides this, massive amounts of general equipment and supplies were shuttled back and forth between South Africa and South West Africa, while later in the war, as South African units penetrated ever deeper into Angola, the lifeblood of the SADF mechanized battalions was supplied largely by air. In addition, much of the support offered to UNITA, South Africa's proxy in the parallel Angolan civil war, was in the form of troop transportation and the movement of heavy armaments and equipment. All this work was done by the pilots of 28 Squadron and their fleet of C-130 Hercules and C-160 Transalls based at AFB Waterkloof.

The acquisition of these aircraft began with an initial purchase of seven Lockheed Hercules C-130B medium transport aircraft from the United States in 1963, which were flown to South Africa by members of 28 Squadron. As the decade ended, however, the transport commitments of the SAAF began to increase commensurate with the growing insecurity on the South West African border with Angola. The transport capacity of 28 Squadron was then augmented further with the acquisition in August 1969 of a small fleet of nine C-160Z Transall aircraft. Both of these aircraft would remain in service, with none being lost, throughout the duration of the Border War and South Africa's involvement in the Angolan civil war. A dedicated study is certainly deserved to chronicle the operational work undertaken by 28 Squadron, arguably the most unsung practitioners of the great art of flying throughout the 23-year conflict.

However, no less important was the introduction into service of four helicopter marques, without which an effective counter-insurgency war of the type ongoing in South West Africa could not have been attempted. The SAAF flew the French Aérospatiale Alouette III and Puma helicopters, to a lesser extent the Aérospatiale Super Frelon and periodically the British Westland Wasp, the former two of which, in particular, would form the backbone of counter-insurgency operations on the ground.

The Alouette III proved itself a highly versatile, robust and adaptable helicopter, also serving the Rhodesians and the Portuguese, the latter using it both in Mozambique and Angola. It first entered service with the French armed forces in 1960, appearing shortly afterward in South Africa with a total of 118 machines being purchased from 1962 until the late 1970s. The early use of the aircraft tended to be in training helicopter pilots and flight engineers, with secondary peacetime uses such as general search and rescue complementing a multiplicity of other day-to-day functions. It was as a fighting platform, however, that the Alouette III really proved its worth. In Rhodesia both Rhodesian and South African Alouettes (the *draadkar*, or 'wire car', as it was euphemistically known) were used in Fire Force deployments on a daily basis, absorbing almost unlimited punishment, some aircraft

A SAAF loadmaster, a 'loadie', tucks into his lunch aboard a C-160 transport. *Photo courtesy Cameron Blake*

The C-160 Transall.

The Alouette III.

SAAF Alouettes IIIs on Fire Force duty in Rhodesia.

A SAAF Alouette III uplifts a stick of SAP operators from a koppie in the Zambezi Valley, Rhodesia, 1968.

amounting to nothing more than a conglomeration of salvaged and spare parts.[2] It was described by some troops as being the 'Land Rover of the Sky', infinitely repairable and as unyielding to personal comfort as human engineering could possibly achieve.

The Alouette III saw ongoing and consistent service in the SAAF during the Border War, serving as a gunship platform, as Fire Force deployment, casevac and as day-to-day troop transports. Alouettes were the first aircraft to enter the South West African theatre and the last to leave. Final formation flights of this legendary fighting machine took place over AFB Bloemspruit on 4 May 2006 and AFB Swartkop on 30 June 2006, after which the Alouette III was officially withdrawn from service.

The Puma SA 330 was an entirely different concept. Not quite the seat-of-the-pants *draadkar* that the Alouette was, it was developed in the 1960s to meet French and British requirements for a tactical medium-transport helicopter with all-weather day-night capabilities.

The SAAF was one of the first export customers to introduce the aircraft into service. The Rhodesians also recognized the potential of this fast, agile and versatile machine for use in the evolving conflict in that country but failed to slip the noose of an arms embargo in time to acquire any. No. 19 Squadron was formed in 1970 to accommodate the new aircraft as pilots began to emerge from training and conversion courses to fly them. In

June 1972 B Flight of 19 Squadron was formed in Durban in order to use the Pumas in search and rescue, a role for which they were also ideally suited.

Several more similar purchases were made right up until the imposition of the mandatory UN-sponsored arms embargo in the late 1970s, which positioned the Puma as the principal muscle of the counter-insurgency war underway in South West Africa. The retractable undercarriage, sleek design and inherent agility, coupled with a 16-man troop-carrying capacity made the Puma ideal for the job. SAAF Pumas were deployed in Rhodesia on numerous occasions for Jumbo Fire Force operations, cross-border raids and other functions. The aircraft were flown by 15 Squadron (Durban), 16 Squadron (Port Elizabeth), 17 Squadron (Pretoria),

19 Squadron (Pretoria/Durban) and 31 Squadron (Hoedspruit).

The role of Pumas in the Border War was extremely varied and included normal trooping, rapid deployment during follow-up, radio relay, casualty evacuation, search and rescue and Special Forces insertion. Up until 1980 it carried a variety of weapons including the ubiquitous mounted 7.62 MAG machine guns, .50-calibre Browning machine guns, 12.5mm gun and side-firing 20mm cannon. In 1986, however, a modification was introduced that had the doors sealed shut in order to accommodate two stub wings capable of carrying the under-nose Kentron TC-20 20mm cannon slaved to a helmet-mounted site, with additional provision for four 68mm rocket pods or anti-tank and air-to-air missiles.[3]

The Super Frelons, also manufactured by Aérospatiale, 16 of which were introduced into service in South Africa, was a three-engine heavy transport helicopter that did not see a great deal of service in the South West African–Angolan theatre thanks to deficiencies discovered in its operation in hot and dry conditions, and at medium to high altitude. It did make occasional appearances however, where it was flown by 30 and 15 squadrons. It was withdrawn from service in 1990 with a patchy service record, being replaced first by the more reliable Puma and later but the adapted Oryx.

The principal training aircraft adopted by the SAAF, although by no means exclusively a training asset, was the, Aermacchi MB 326M, a local variant of which was produced under licence by the Atlas Aircraft Corporation, and known as the Impala Mk I. The Impala Mk II was followed soon after, taking to the air in 1974.

A brief word on this unremarkable-looking light strike fighter would be a suitable end to this chapter. A small force of Impalas was used in the air war, becoming indispensable in a variety of roles, with reconnaissance being perhaps the most notable of these. In areas adjacent to Angola and South West Africa, where the Border War proper was fought, visual reconnaissance was carried out by Impalas in search of suspect activity for ground forces to follow up on. During these sorties the Impalas were formidably armed with the ubiquitous 68mm SNEB rockets and 30mm cannon in order to engage with enemy positions or vehicles whenever they were encountered.

Impalas also performed less glamorous work in support of ground troops, reconnaissance teams and other aircraft in external operations as airborne radio relay points – Telstar operations as they were known – and general close air support (CAS) during which pilots would wait in full readiness, often in cockpit standby, in order to provide rapid assistance to Special Force reconnaissance units operating in Angola or counter-insurgency operations in the border areas. This was tedious work when things were quiet but extremely exacting and valuable to the general war effort when they were not.

CHAPTER TWO:
THE BEGINNING: OPERATION *BLOUWILDEBEES* AND THE START OF THE BORDER WAR

The 1960s was an active time on the southern African revolutionary front. A rapid evolution of local black nationalist/liberation movements took place across the board with the formation of countless congresses, political parties and revolutionary fronts wherever resistance to decolonization presaged war. In southern Africa the key dominoes to fall were Tanzania, Zaire and Zambia, each of which offered rear bases for the further assault on the hardest nuts to crack: Angola, Mozambique, Rhodesia and South West Africa. South Africa would fall by economic sanctions and diplomatic pressure. No movement, not least the South African ANC, was under any illusion that that particular edifice would topple as a consequence of armed rebellion.

South Africa, however, was the military force that would confront the liberation movement for Namibia, SWAPO, or the South West African People's Organization, the last of the great southern African armed revolutionary movements to press forward the struggle and the last to prevail.

SWAPO was very much cut from the cloth of regional nationalist liberation movements, each of which represented the evolution of much association-forming and modern political orientation, all of which also coincided with the emergence of the first generation of young and radical black intelligentsia. Prior to this, black political language had tended to be restrained and organizations on the whole were law-abiding and sought, rather than to overthrow white minority rule, to work to ameliorate the poor social and wage conditions of blacks from within the system. The progressive toppling of colonial rule farther north generally had a radicalizing effect on the youth of the southern African region who, competently led for the most part, began to agitate with increasing violence for full political independence.

In the 1960s this low-level violence rarely exceeded what might be regarded as civil disturbance and was dealt with by the civil authority backed up when necessary by emergency powers. This gradually began to transmute into an armed struggle as political links were established between the various nationalist leaderships and Eastern bloc countries, in particular China and the Soviet Union, but many others at various times. This resulted in the training and arming of guerrilla movements and the establishment of rear bases in friendly liberated countries as part of the unofficial mandate of the so-called Front Line States and

A close-up of the results of a Cessna's PR.

the more formalized policy of the Organization of African Unity.

The active zones of insecurity throughout the late 1960s and early 1970s were focused on Rhodesia, Mozambique and Angola, the former being under the control of a white rebel government and the latter pair being governed in the Portuguese style as overseas provinces. In the case of Mozambique the local dynamics were reasonably straightforward. FRELIMO was an authentic, Marxist-orientated unity movement representing all the indigenous peoples of the territory and bonded by the charismatic and strong leadership of Samora Machel. In Angola, however, matters were a great deal more opaque. The liberation struggle here took form from a number of regional and ethnic threads that coalesced eventually into three separate and constituted but mutually antagonistic liberation movements. It therefore stood to reason that the war of liberation was really nothing more than the first phase of a civil war that would not be decided until the Portuguese had left the scene, after which matters could be concluded between the three opposing nationalist movements.

The senior and arguably the most politically radical of these movements was the MPLA, the People's Movement for the Liberation of Angola, centred around and ethnically supported within the capital of Luanda. Representing the north of Angola and overlapping into recently independent Zaire, was the right-leaning FNLA, or the National Liberation Front of Angola. A breakaway faction of this organization was the National Union for the Total Independence of Angola, or UNITA, centred in the southeast of the country, pro-west and ideologically irreconcilable with either the MPLA or the FNLA.

So long as the Portuguese held substantive political control of Angola, all that fundamentally concerned South Africa with regard to the security of her long-shared proxy border with Angola was the threat posed by SWAPO which, although extremely scrappy and highly militant in terms of its language and posturing, could do little more than irritate South African border security from its rear bases in Zambia. A glance at a map of the region will illustrate this fact clearly. The 1,000 kilometres or more of arid frontier that separates present-day Namibia from its northern neighbours is only touched by Zambia at the far end of the Caprivi Strip. This invited SWAPO combatants to either challenge the South Africans at their point of strength around the four corners of Zambia, Rhodesia and Botswana or to infiltrate Angola overland the entire length of the frontier to Owamboland on the northwestern edge of the country in order to merge with the ethnically sympathetic Owambo who provided the bedrock of support for SWAPO. And while this was possible, it hardly offered a platform for a serious military challenge and indeed no such challenge was ever really offered.

SWAPO, in keeping with the liberation ideology of Mao, from which many in the region drew their tactical inspiration, forswore trading punches with a dominant army entrenched in its territorial heartland but instead focused on the wider politicization of masses in a battle for hearts and minds, a battle that white South African youth, conscripted for the most part from the industrial and urban centres of South Africa, had lost before they had even reached the border.

In fact, during the early phases of the Border War, the fighting was not army business at all, but a police affair. This was also the case in similar situations elsewhere. There was always a marked reluctance on the part of any colonial authority to acknowledge that local insecurity was anything more than a civil disturbance. If an internal insurgency could be dealt with primarily by the civil power then it need not be defined as a war, which in turn criminalized violent political activity in the countryside which tended to rob it of the legitimacy of protest.

Such was the case in South West Africa, with responsibility for confronting the insurgency falling not to the SADF, which retained a presence in the region and acted only when requested to do so in support of the South West African Police (SWAPOL).

For the most part the police incident reports that were filed tended to paint a picture of the usual hit-and-run-type insecurity involving isolated and vulnerable targets such as the widely dispersed white farmsteads or white-owned rural stores, with frequent killings of local chiefs and other blacks perceived to be loyal to the government. Very seldom was an attack recorded against a defended government facility and even less frequently against any part of the defence establishment itself. Police and army casualties were most frequently caused by landmines which were easily laid and difficult to detect and were the preferred offensive weapon of insurgent units. Large numbers of police personnel, and perhaps even more civilians, were killed or maimed by the widespread use of landmines.

The South African Police response tended to involve wide-ranging reconnaissance patrols that rarely succeeded in running mobile insurgent units to ground but kept them on the move, preventing the establishment of any permanent or semi-permanent facilities within South West Africa. Portuguese military activity in Angola had limited effect even on its own internal enemies, let alone SWAPO, but friendly entente between the two territories did at least prevent SWAPO from gaining any permanent foothold in that country.

Air support for police patrols and counter-insurgency operations was provided by two seconded SAAF Alouette IIIs, one of which was lost in April 1966 during a night flight when the pilot strayed over the ocean.

The point at which this level of insecurity escalated to something more akin to war was in August 1966 when a combined SWAPOL/SADF/SAAF operation codenamed Operation *Blouwildebees* took the fight to the enemy in Angola. Intelligence reports during February/March 1966 indicated the presence near the Luenge National Park in Angola of a large unit of SWAPO preparing to move into the politically alert Owamboland region of South West Africa, having exfiltrated Zambia and made its way westward along the extended frontier. The matter was investigated and confirmed. An operation was then tabled to deal with the group, scheduled for 26 August 1966.

The plan involved a simple airborne assault on the known location of the group, utilizing an additional six Alouette IIIs flown by pilots trained specifically to operate without flight engineers. This was in order to allow for a complement of six fully-equipped police reaction force personnel or army paratroops which would not have been possible with the addition of a flight technician on board. Each helicopter was adapted to allow troops to exit on a knotted rope should the thick woodland of the target area prevent a landing. This required the pilot, while flying with his right hand, to retrieve the rope with his left. The operation involved three administrative branches of the defence establishment and was commanded respectively by Brigadier Jan Blaauw for the SAAF, General Pat Dillon for the police and Brigadier Renfree and Major Paetzold for the SADF.

The small armada of seven helicopters took to the air at zero hour and navigated carefully toward the target, following the directional advice of an informer. The drops occurred largely without mishap, after which a brief but ferocious firefight ensued against a dug-in and spirited, although largely outclassed enemy.

The enemy was armed primarily with the venerable but rather obsolete Soviet World War-era PPSh-41 sub-machine gun that fired a 7.62 pistol round which could hardly be effective against the hard-punching South African RIs (FAL variant) fielded by the assault force and neither, for that matter, the airborne mounted machine guns that in fact accounted for most of the enemy deaths that day. Bows and arrows also happen to have been found on the scene but these, it was later established, were not intended as offensive weapons but for hunting purposes in a situation where random gunfire would obviously have been inadvisable.

Once the dust had settled and a brief in-situ interrogation of the surviving guerrillas completed, it was established that a number had managed to escape, their trenches having being fortunately situated outside of the drop circle. Four helicopters were soon airborne and scouring the surrounding bush for evidence of the fugitives. Three were located and engaged from the air, resulting in the death of one and capture of the other two. The net haul of the operation was two killed and another seriously injured, with eight captured. Upon this modest result Operation *Blouwildebees* was wound down and the six additional helicopters flown to Rooikop AFB, from where they were ferried by C-130s back to South Africa and AFB Swartkop.

The next aircraft to find itself on border operations in South West Africa was that old South African standard of the East and North African campaigns of the Second World War: the North American 'Harvard' Trainers of 8 Squadron, based in AFB Bloemspruit, Bloemfontein. Eight of these aircraft were flown north in relays to AFB Rundu on the southern bank of the Okavango River for the purpose of providing top cover and escorts for a heliborne assault to be staged against a meeting of high-level SWAPO leaders due to take place some 130 kilometres north of Rundu in a place called Sacatxai close the Angolan town of Mavinga. The plan was for police to seal off the meeting and capture as many of the guerrilla leaders as possible. All insignia had been painted over and the Harvards, traditionally a training craft, were geared up for war. The operation was bungled, however, due to a misplaced troop drop that even when rectified gave the intended targets ample time to pack up and flee. The camp was destroyed and the airborne force deployed back to AFB Rundu.

What is perhaps most interesting about this operation was not so much its details or the lack of success, but that it was the first aggressive sortie into Angola by fixed-wing aircraft and, moreover, that it should have been these particular aircraft involved. South Africa certainly had supersonic fighters available for deployment at that time, with the Mirage III fleet beginning to enter service as early as 1963 and the MB-326M Impala Mk I becoming operational late in 1966. However, the careful removal of insignia might indicate a certain amount of caution in exposing South African aircraft to easy identification in Angola where South African involvement had not yet been officially acknowledged. The South African government was extremely tight-lipped about military support given to the Portuguese in Angola but the practical advantages of this were obvious, with the SAAF providing helicopter and light transport assistance in a number of Portuguese military operations.

It is also worth mentioning in this context that a low-key South African military/police presence in Rhodesia had been in place since mid-1967. This was authorized as a consequence of a brief and ill-advised alliance between the guerrillas of the South African ANC armed wing, *Umkhonto we Sizwe* (MK), and units of Rhodesian ZAPU, which resulted in a rolling security force operation, Operation *Nickel*, that ultimately accounted for all involved. This alerted South Africa to renewed attempts by MK to utilize insecurity in Rhodesia to infiltrate armed and trained

A Harvard, insignia removed and geared up for war.

An SAP Cessna 185 at a forward airfield in Rhodesia in 1967, just prior to all South African aircraft being camouflaged.

is suggestive of the fact that a great many more South African ships than this were involved. South African Pumas and Super Frelons also saw periodic service in Rhodesia.

In the meanwhile, the most concentrated and important work done by the SAAF during the early months and years of the South West African SWAPO insurgency was in the comprehensive aerial mapping of the operational zones with a view to updating a wholly inadequate topographical understanding of the region, defined then by little more than the standard commercially available Michelin road maps. Most of this work was undertaken between 1972 and 1974 and was mainly the responsibility of SAAF 12 Squadron, a light-bomber squadron formed in 1939, primarily for service in the East and North African theatres, being disbanded at the end of the Second World War after having been employed in the valedictory task of transporting South African servicemen back home. It was briefly reformed in 1946 for the role of tsetse-fly control in Zululand and northern Natal and then as a helicopter squadron flying the early Sikorsky S-51, before being merged as a flight of the medium-transport 28 Squadron. With the introduction into service in 1963 of the superb English Electric Canberra bomber, however, the squadron was once again re-formed to fly these aircraft which saw service in the SAAF until 1991 in high-altitude reconnaissance and, of course, in photo-reconnaissance.

Photo-reconnaissance missions were fairly wide-ranging and not limited to the South West African border region but extended at times to cover Angola as far north as Cabinda, the entirety of Mozambique and large areas of Tanzania, including Dar es Salaam. Raw footage was received and organized at the Joint Air Reconnaissance and Intelligence Centre situated at AFB Waterkloof from which a series of detailed photomaps was produced that would prove vital in the planning of precise operations as the pace of war escalated.

cadres into South Africa, which in turn resulted in the deployment in Rhodesia of some 2,000 SAP members posing as riot police and supported by SAAF helicopters. It is also worth noting that direct South African military support in Rhodesia, in particular in the matter of air assets, was ongoing and tended to run hot and cold depending on the South African political mood at any given time. The most important tool of Rhodesian counter-insurgency warfare, as it was for South Africa's own growing insurgency, was the ubiquitous Alouette III, and although no accurate records exist to indicate how many of these were in service in Rhodesia, a figure of 50-plus has been suggested by historians Paul Moorcraft and Peter McLaughlin in their book *The Rhodesian War*. According to Rhodesian military historian Dr J.R.T. Wood, 24 of these were on loan from South Africa. The fact that, in 1980, the incoming Zimbabwean government took possession of a mere eight functioning Alouettes once the dust had settled

CHAPTER THREE:
OPERATION *SAVANNAH*: SAAF IN A SUPPORT ROLE

"The events of 1974–75 prompted a belated assertion of US
regional influence to stem further violence and polarization and
to pre-empt further Soviet exploitation of regional strife"
—Chester Crocker

The sudden abandonment by the Portuguese of their overseas provinces after a 1974 military coup in Lisbon took a great many people at the higher echelons of government by surprise. South African minister of defence, and later president of the republic, P.W. Botha, was quoted in the press only a month before the coup in Lisbon as doubting whether the Portuguese would ever consider abandoning their grip on Mozambique and Angola, bearing in mind the 400-year history of their occupation. This comment contrasted sharply with local intelligence assessments but was forgivable perhaps for the fact that in diplomatic circles, at least, the Portuguese had so sustained their imperial hubris that few could have doubted their determination to hang on. Lisbon fell silent on the matter only once the determinedly blind fascist government of Marcello Caetano had fallen, at which point the abrupt reality of a strategic power vacuum in central Africa became starkly apparent to all.

The simple facts of the situation are thus: the Portuguese had for some time been losing ground militarily in all three major African theatres, in particular in Mozambique, with a discernible discontent and lethargy affecting the armed forces as the death toll mounted and territorial losses accrued. To many in the ranks of the *Exército Português*, the army, upon whom the brunt of attrition was focused, the economic and human cost of attempting to retain control of Portugal's overseas territories was simply too high. The government was therefore toppled in a leftist military coup on 25 April 1974, with the abrupt ending of all colonial wars becoming perhaps the highest item on the new national agenda.

Independence for Mozambique and Angola was not immediate, but it was de facto upon the formality of a negotiated, and rushed, handover. This left very little time for those with an interest in the outcome of the process to try and influence it. For Rhodesia and South Africa the prospect of a communist takeover in two such vast entities as Mozambique and Angola was unnerving in the extreme, but on a broader stage the Cold War ramifications of such a power vacuum energized both the United States and the Soviet Union – including Cuba as a nominal proxy of the USSR – to act.

In practical terms the matter of a power vacuum tended to affect Mozambique less than it did Angola. There was no doubt that FRELIMO would assume power in Mozambique, and with the Castroesque Samora Machel at the helm of government, its Marxist orientation was also never in doubt. In Angola, on the other hand, the future remained to be settled, be it by negotiation or war, with the latter being the preferred option of each faction if the former failed. With understandable pragmatism, all sides tended to settle on the notion that an expanded war in the region was not only inevitable but in some ways desirable too. (Holden Roberto, leader of the FNLA and a brother-in-law of Zaire's Mobuto, retained the position, rhetorically at least, that his ambition extended no further than an independent baKongo homeland in the north of Angola.)

Of the two superpowers it was the Soviet Union which was quicker off the mark, arriving in the region ahead of the United States with its support of the MPLA, the most left-leaning of all three of the Angolan revolutionary movements and the one centred on the capital Luanda, which tended to give it the best chance of ultimately seizing power.

The United States, extremely gun-shy in the aftermath of events in Vietnam, was very reluctant to commit troops to southern Africa and felt more inclined to solicit the help of South Africa, an ideological if not a political ally, in influencing events on the ground to the benefit of the West. At the time this was music to South African ears and, although militarily not quite as muscular as it would later become, the South African government felt confident that something practical could be achieved. This, in simple terms, was the backdrop to Operation *Savannah*, the first unequivocal plunge by the South African military establishment into war in Angola.

US diplomat and Assistant Secretary of State for African Affairs from 1981 to 1989, Chester Crocker, defined the situation on the ground extremely well as Angola began to count down the days to the agreed date of independence from Portugal.

By November 11, 1975, the date of independence, Angola had been effectively thrown to the wolves and a feeding frenzy was underway. Cuban, South African and Zairean combat troops had intervened directly. Mercenaries, advisers and air force and armour crews were engaged from such countries as Algeria, Britain, China, Cuba, France, the Netherlands, Portugal, South Africa, West Germany, the Soviet Union and the United States. Arms and financial support came principally from France, the United States, China, Czechoslovakia, Cuba, Belgium, Nigeria, South Africa, Saudi Arabia and the USSR. The interventions came from land, sea and air; Angola's notional 'territorial integrity' was violated from the Atlantic and from facilities in Zaire, Congo, Guinea, Guinea-Bissau, Mali, Zambia and South African-controlled Namibia.[4]

SAAF Canberra crews, 1975.

WO Ken van Straaten, the SAAF's most decorated NCO, mans an MAG in the door of a helicopter.

A flight of Canberras

A Bosbok light reconnaissance aircraft over Owamboland.

The rationale behind the South African decision to get involved in this Gordian knot to the extent that it was not obvious lies beyond the scope of this narrative. Suffice to say that in early August 1975, at a time more or less corresponding with the arrival in Angola of several thousand Cuban troops, MPLA forces aggressively began to move southward along the coast, in due course threatening the Ruacana–Calueque hydroelectric complex, a joint Angolan–South African venture and a vital water-supply project for the arid and underdeveloped Owamboland region of South West Africa. Part of the facility was inside Angola and, once South African technical staff began to be menaced, the SADF responded by moving 50 kilometres in-country and forcefully occupying the town of Calueque.

This was in early August 1975. At midnight on 15 October the SADF Task Force Zulu, the first of a number of battle groups that would in due course become involved, and comprising Alpha and Bravo groups, crossed from South West Africa into Cuando Cubango, Angola, ostensibly in support of the pro-West FNLA and UNITA, but in effect to roll back the significant territorial advances being made by the MPLA and, moreover, to attempt to affect the outcome of the internal power struggle in the country prior to the date of independence. The decision was made to some extent in spite of deep misgivings felt by Prime Minister John Vorster – or this is at least what was widely reported – but based also on considerable pressure being applied to South Africa from

such friendly African governments as Côte d'Ivoire, Zaire and Zambia, and an 'understanding' on the matter reached with the United States.[5]

By any standards the advance of the combined South African force northward into Angola ranks as one of the great epics of mobile warfare in Africa, not dissimilar to the comprehensive Allied rout of the Italians in Somalia and Ethiopia during the East Africa Campaign of the Second World War, during which, incidentally, large numbers of South African troops and armoured and air force assets also took part. An ambulating and apparently unstoppable two-pronged advance saw the South Africans move north over vast swathes of Angolan territory, mounted in many instances in an assortment of requisitioned refugee transports, Eland armoured cars, Unimogs and Land Rovers, and aside from a handful of stirring actions, encountering very little organized resistance. In 33 days the SADF advanced an extraordinary 3,159 kilometres, engaging in 30 attacks and 21 skirmishes, killing a conservative tally of 210 enemy troops, wounding a further 96 and securing some 56 captures, weighed against the loss of five South African soldiers and 41 wounded. This, bearing in mind that most fighting men involved were irregulars, was an astonishing achievement.[6]

The SAAF played a very limited role in the operation. Apart from a long-range Canberra bombing sortie, flown to support elements of the FNLA under Holden Roberto during an ill-

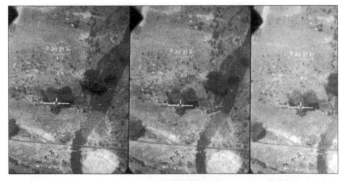

An attack on a bush target seen through a camera-gun sight.

advised attempt to capture Luanda from the north on the eve of the national independence – the disastrous Battle of Quifangondo – the distances were found to be too great for the deployment of useful offensive operations in support of ground troops. Instead Cessna 185 aircraft were used in a light communication role and, of course, the ubiquitous Puma helicopter was consistently deployed in battlefield support, with one ship being recorded lost, taken down on 22 December 1975 by anti-aircraft artillery originating from a hillside some 18 kilometres northwest of Cela in the Cuanza Sul Province. In this instance, the pilot and crew effected a successful forced landing after which, some 50 kilometres ahead of the SADF farthest north, evaded capture for 22 hours before finding their way back to safety.

Such was not the case a few weeks earlier when a C-185 spotter aircraft was shot down over Ebo, also in the Cuanza Sul Province, during the tense battle for that town. Two pilots and an air observer were killed in what transpired as the first de facto defeat of the advance. Despite many efforts in the aftermath of this incident, the remains of the three aircrew have never been recovered.

The area in which the SAAF provided invaluable support was in air transport and resupply. Here the heavy lifting was undertaken mainly by the pilots and crews of 28 Squadron, shuttling the squadron fleet of ever-dependable C-160 Transall and C-130 Hercules transporters back and forth from Angolan airstrips, carrying personnel, ammunition, rations and casualty evacuations. At one point it was recorded that the transport fleet was operating out of the Cela airfield more or less on a 24-hour basis, with one crew registering over 100 hours of flight time over a 12-day period, significantly more than the legal limit.

Ultimately the South African advance was halted by a combination of bridges destroyed by retreating enemy and a rapid escalation of Cuban military support for the MPLA and its military wing FAPLA. It is also fair to say that a severe bout of political jitters affecting previously committed regimes, not least among them the United States, contributed much to a change of heart in Pretoria. The question now had to be asked: what would South Africa have done with Luanda should it have succeeded in taking the city? She could hardly have hoped to occupy Angola and certainly she would not have been able to hold onto the capital city for long. Moreover, the unpublished US guarantees and promises that had inspired Pretoria to undertake such an ambitious military expedition were now clearly no longer relevant, and with much lowing in the OAU pen regarding the legitimacy of the MPLA, and with a general acceptance internationally that this was so, there seemed little point in South Africa leaning further out on a limb to make a bad job good. Castro, it seemed, had dramatically raised the stakes on behalf of the Soviet bloc, called the bluff of the West and had won. Angola now lay within the Soviet–Cuban sphere of influence and there was nothing for it but for South Africa to effect an orderly withdrawal, conceding each district back to the MPLA as it did.

The best that could be said about it all was that South Africa now had a new regional ally in UNITA which, in fairness, was scant compensation for the loss of an old regional ally in Portugal and the arrival of SWAPO in liberated Angola with all the material and moral support that the MPLA and the Cubans and Soviets could offer. The FNLA had effectively dissipated in the aftermath of the disastrous defeat at Battle of Quifangondo which, incidentally, saw the South African support contingent evacuated from the coastal town of Ambrizete, some 150 kilometres north of Luanda, using inflatables and a SAAF Westland Wasp helicopter to shuttle men on board the SAS *President Steyn* in a combined South African naval and air force operation.

CHAPTER FOUR:
THE COLLAPSE OF PORTUGUESE RULE IN AFRICA: A NEW ERA AND A NEW ENEMY

Perhaps the most important lesson to be absorbed by South Africa in the aftermath of *Savannah* was how disadvantaged in the matter of equipment, armour and technology the defence establishment was after some 30 years of military malaise. The campaign had illustrated very clearly the limitations of guts and glory in the face of the sophisticated Soviet weaponry that was pouring into Angola and into the hands of FAPLA front-line units. South African artillerymen, as only one example, had on more than one occasion during Operation *Savannah* found themselves comprehensively outranged by their opponents and had only managed to keep one step ahead thanks to excellent training and very nimble tactics. The same was true in terms of air support, armoured vehicles and tanks, all of which prompted military planners at home to begin to give serious thought to plugging the gaps.

The difficulty, of course, was that South Africa was finding herself increasing constricted by the United Nations arms

Line-up of Mirage IIIEZ and twin-seat D2Z aircraft at AFB Pietersburg.

Anti-missile flares being ejected from a Mirage F1AZ.

embargo and a general unwillingness on the part of key global arms suppliers to deal with the country. Britain, with its titanic post-colonial conscience, was among the first to restrict arms supplies to South Africa – ironic, many were apt to grumble, bearing in mind that South Africa had managed to overcome a natural aversion to the British in order to defend her empire in two world wars. South Africa, however, owned a fledgling arms industry which, ironically again, owed its existence to British encouragement and capital and which had produced a considerable amount of support matériel for the general Second World War Allied effort.

South Africa had begun, as we have heard, to fall from grace in the aftermath of the 1948 general election that introduced the National Party into power and which began the process of institutionalized apartheid that the global community would in due course begin to find so unpalatable. This increasingly negative sentiment on the part of various global forums peaked as a consequence of the March 1960 Sharpeville Massacre that saw some 69 blacks gunned down by police during an anti-pass law demonstration. The United Nations was finally nudged awake from an unquiet slumber over the matter of creeping South African race dichotomy and began issuing ever-more shrill edicts condemning the regime and encouraging voluntary international sanctions, in particular an arms embargo.

That Britain was among the first to respond perhaps goes some way to explain the South African choice of the French aircraft manufacturer Dassault Aviation for the acquisition of the substantial fleet of Mirage IIIs and F1s. The former were acquired in the early 1960s and included CZ interceptors, EZ ground-attack, BZ and DZ dual-seat trainers as well as photo-reconnaissance RZ versions of the aircraft. The decision to acquire an additional fleet of F1s was taken in 1969 but these did not begin to arrive in South Africa until 1975 and were unavailable at the time of Operation *Savannah*. The jet fighter force in fact only deployed permanently during the latter phases of the Border War, namely between 1978 and 1988.

In the meanwhile, an armaments production board had been established in 1964 for the purpose of controlling and monitoring general arms procurement, supply and manufacture for the SADF,

South Africa at that point having shed the Union and established itself as a republic. Four years later the Industrial Development Corporation helped to establish a parastatal entity, the Armaments Development and Production Corporation, or Armscor, tasked with bringing together the many disparate elements of production, to establish new branches where needed and to oversee all arms imports and exports.

As the 1970s progressed international resolve against South Africa intensified. The mandatory arms embargo imposed by the United Nations in 1976, as had been the case with Rhodesia a decade earlier, simply had the effect of spurring local innovation and production and the quest for unorthodox markets and irregular partnerships. One of these was a strategic defence cooperation agreement with Israel that saw South African troops appearing in the field armed with Israeli Galil assault rifles, later replaced by the South African R4 assault rifle, a licensed variant of the Galil which came into service in 1982. Prior to this, South African troops had been armed with the R1 assault rifle, itself a licensed variant of the *Fabrique Nationale* FN FAL which was also supplied in large numbers to sanctions-constrained Rhodesia to the north.

It was during the 1980s that the South African Border War escalated and internationalized to the extent that it essentially became a conventional war. This, in combination with the international mood of the anti-apartheid movement, further constrained South Africa's ability to source military matériel abroad. The 1980s was also a period of intense militarization within South Africa as the breadth and scope of the Border War spread and as the domestic arms industry began to produce a wider range of ever-more sophisticated weaponry and support equipment.

There were many examples of this. One such example is the development of the Olifant tank which was the result of a series of upgrades of the British Centurion tank, undertaken in part in cooperation with Israel that similarly used modified Centurions in its *Sho't* programme. In the same way the Atlas Cheetah, produced by the Atlas Aircraft Corporation, was merely a home-grown upgrade of a Mirage III, evolving through several variants and resembling very closely the Israel Aircraft Industries *Kfir*,

An SADF NCO barks out orders during a contact in the border area. *Photo courtesy Cameron Blake*

FAPLA BM-21 multiple-rocket launcher in action.

An SADF patrol along the cut-line. *Photo courtesy Cameron Blake*

The G6.

which was itself based on a Mirage V. Other aircraft produced locally by Atlas Aircraft Corporation, a key component industry of Armscor, were the Atlas Oryx, a medium-sized utility helicopter which began its development process as an Aérospatiale SA 330 Puma conversion, the Impala Mk I, an Italian Aermacchi MB-326 variant built in South Africa under licence, and the Bosbok and Kudu, Italian-designed light utility aircraft that saw consistent service throughout the Border War.

Perhaps the most iconic item of South African mechanized infantry hardware is the six-wheel-drive Ratel IFV, a highly versatile and adaptable infantry fighting vehicle which, in keeping with the customary lineage of many South African innovations, arrived on the drawing board once the fleet of British FV603 Alvis Saracens in service in the SADF ceased to be viable once spare parts became unobtainable. Design work on the Ratel variants began in 1968 with the first prototypes being completed in 1974. Production by Sandock-Austral began in 1976 with the first vehicles being introduced into service the following year. Another cornerstone product was the G5 155mm howitzer which came into being to correct the disadvantages suffered by South African artillerymen outranged on the battlefield by sophisticated

Soviet-supplied heavy guns. The G6 self-propelled howitzer was developed around the ordnance of the G5 but with a motorized and mine-protected wheeled chassis. During Operation *Savannah* the South Africans had been exposed to the highly intimidating 122mm BM-21 rocket launcher, the Stalin Organ of popular battlefield mythology, which, although proving itself to have more bark than bite, nonetheless was copied by the South Africans from a captured model to produce the 127mm Valkiri multiple-rocket launcher.

The list of South African-innovated, -pirated and -produced battlefield hardware is long but is perhaps best defined by an anecdote related to the development of a South African-produced flight helmet. The first hostile encounters over the skies of Angola with enemy MiGs gave added impetus to the development of the South African V3 series of air-to-air missiles which were designed to be integrated with a helmet-mounted sight, also of South African design. Development of the helmets began in 1975 with the SAAF being the first air force to fly operationally with this type of system. However, one of these helmets was stolen by Soviet spy and ex-South Africa Navy commodore Dieter Gerhardt who duly passed it over to his handlers. In later years, once South African

The formidable South African G5.

A G5 in action.

often led to direct contact or intelligence build-ups that allowed for more orchestrated infantry or airborne actions to take place. Alongside this, covert military support continued to be given to UNITA in respect of the fact that the organization, if not advancing South African interests by its own agenda, was at least hostile to SWAPO and a force multiplier in a situation where politics often proscribed the limits of South African military action. In this type of action the SAAF returned to its support role, with the transport pilots of 28 Squadron doing the usual heavy lifting, the Kudus and Bosboks plying the cut-line on Telstar (airborne radio relay) duty and the Pumas and Alouettes backing up the troops in the field with vital supply, deployment and casevac. The Bosboks and Kudus also undertook air reconnaissance, target-marking, casevac, liaison duties and countless other mundane tasks essential in maintaining an effective air operation.

The Mirages only arrived on the scene during 1978 once the difficult political decision had been made to permit what the military men had been urging for some time: to take the war to the enemy by mounting aggressive cross-border raids in the same way that the Rhodesians were doing in Mozambique and Zambia, cutting the enemy to pieces where he was concentrated and dealing with him before he had a chance to infiltrate the country.

The difficulty in making this decision lay in the fact that, notwithstanding many grotesque battlefield and politicization practices, the revolutionary–guerrilla organizations held the moral high ground by dint of their particular place in history, and could be relied upon to make optimum use of any propaganda coup that the South Africans might offer them by focusing their (the South African) operational superiority on the business of killing 'gooks' in large numbers. Such was the case during the Battle of Cassinga where the SADF in combination with the SAAF delivered SWAPO, and by extension FAPLA, a mauling of such intensity that it is arguable if the organization ever fully recovered. The political fallout was indeed shrill and highly embellished, and the South African reputation was certainly further damaged, but the fact remained that patrolling the border could ultimately achieve nothing like the sort of kill rates that a combined operation could achieve against an unsuspecting guerrilla rear base.

The action at Cassinga was part of a larger operation codenamed *Reindeer* that sought to eliminate a widely dispersed selection of SWAPO bases as well as a much larger concentration focused around the old iron mining town of Cassinga, codenamed *Moscow* by SWAPO, and pioneered as a joint venture between

isolation had been lifted and diplomatic relations normalized, it was found that the helmet sight in operational use by the Russian Air Force was basically that stolen from the South Africans.

All this was in preparation for a rapidly evolving battlefield dynamic. By the dawn of 1976, the MPLA was in effective control of the government and the lion's share of the territorial expanse of Angola. The FNLA was no longer a force of any particular consequence while UNITA, under the charismatic leadership of Jonas Savimbi, remained in existence but savagely depleted in the aftermath of the South African withdrawal.

UNITA clung to a limited swath of territory in the remote south/central provinces of Angola, overlapping the ethnic heartland of the Ovimbundu group, in effect establishing a separate government with its capital in Huambo, Nova Lisboa of yore, and a key centre on the strategically important Benguela railway line that linked the Atlantic port of Lobito to the interior.

In the meanwhile, South African military activity along the border remained for all intents and purposes a classic, low-level counter-insurgency containment. Routine foot and vehicle patrols augmented by deep-penetration reconnaissance were the tool of choice. Here the skills of the individual hunter/killer operative

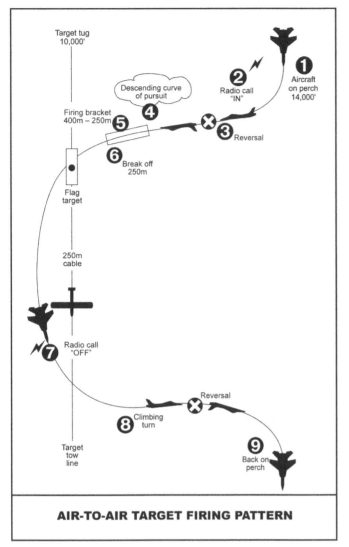

AIR-TO-AIR TARGET FIRING PATTERN

The first SAAF air-to-air training camp was undertaken by 3 Squadron flying Mirage F1s out of AFB Langebaanweg in November 1975.

Paratroopers jumping from the side doors of a C-130 Hercules.

Impala pilots posing with one of their aircraft. From left: Robbie Robinson, Johan du Plessis, Ronnie Knott-Craig, Cobus Toerien, Steyn Venter, Gene Kotze.

the Portuguese authorities and the German Krupp family. The town is situated some 250 kilometres within Angola and had been identified as a key SWAPO forward operational headquarters with the capacity to hold upward of 1,200 combatants. The plan to capture it involved a combined airstrike and Parabat assault against a well-fortified and well-defended position, with the 250 earmarked troops being airlifted out after the operation by an armada of helicopters.

This was a risky proposition by any estimation and for any number of reasons, key among them being the distance involved and the potential for a military and political disaster if things turned conspicuously awry. Complicating matters was the fact that a substantial force of tanks and mechanized infantry belonging to FAPLA and supported by an undetermined number of Cubans was stationed at Techamutete, just 16 kilometres to the south. In addition, it was quite conceivable that the Angolan MiG-21s, known to be in operation, might attempt to intervene.

This, however, was precisely the sort of work that the SAAF Mirage squadrons were itching to get a grip on, and in fact 2 Squadron, the erstwhile Flying Cheetahs of the Korean War, and equipped with Mirage IIIs, had been training intensively for several months in anticipation of a call to the border.

The assault on Cassinga was scheduled for 4 May 1978. The main SAAF attack force would consist of Canberra bombers and 24 Squadron Blackburn Buccaneers which would deliver the first payload of ordnance to soften up the target before the arrival of the C-130s and C-160s of 28 Squadron carrying the paratroops, followed by helicopter uplift. Helicopters would operate and refuel from an established HAA, or helicopter administration area, known more commonly as a HAG, for the Afrikaans *helikopter administrasie gebeid*, which would be established a safe distance from the scene of the action. Top cover would be provided by the Mirage IIIs of 2 Squadron.

At 08h00 on 4 May, four laden Canberras appeared over the ramshackle but heavily fortified settlement of Cassinga onto which was voided a blanket of anti-personnel alpha bombs, followed by the pinpoint delivery of eight hard-hitting 1,000lb bombs by a flight of five Buccaneers.[7] The initial air attack achieved absolute surprise and was so effective that enemy defensive reaction was temporarily paralyzed. This was fortunate for two reasons. Firstly, the question of anti-aircraft artillery remained an open one, answered somewhat later when it was established that in fact Cassinga was well provided for in this regard; these, however, thanks to the shock of the first assault, where not brought to bear in any meaningful way against the vulnerable bomber and transport fleet. In the second instance, it gave South African paratroops an opportunity to regroup after a potentially disastrous off-target drop which resulted in many paratroopers needing to ford a river before going into action.

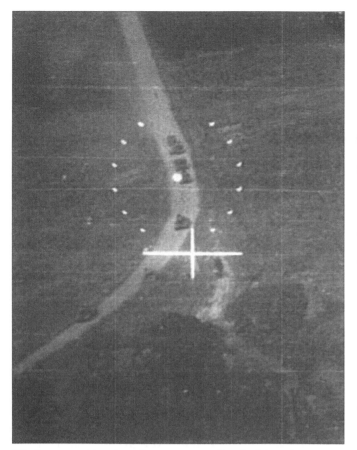

This frame was taken from the gun-camera film of a 2 Squadron Mirage III attacking the armoured column sent to assist the defenders of Cassinga. The pilot was Commandant Ollie Holmes, the squadron commander. Notice the vehicles below his sight picture. These were the ones attacked by Gerrie Radloff.

The sight picture is blurred due to the vibration from the 30mm Defa cannons. The white bursts clearly show the effects of the cannon fire.

One of the four Mirage IIIs armed for air combat and supplying top cover for the operation was summoned to provide close air support against an enemy position firing heavily on advancing troops. The exact position could not be located, however, and fearing a friendly fire incident the attack was aborted. By 14h00 the ground action was largely over with most key objectives attained. At least 600 SWAPO personnel, but possibly as many as 1,000, lay dead, with many more captured and a great deal of intelligence material, although admittedly not as much as hoped, gathered. Soon afterward the helicopter extraction, utilizing 13 Pumas and six Super Felons from 19 Squadron, began. It was at that moment that the anticipated Cuban/FAPLA armoured column was spotted moving cautiously toward Cassinga from the south.

The Mirage IIIs that had earlier returned to AFB Ondangwa were immediately scrambled to offer fighter assistance. (A further two Mirage IIIs had been involved in attacks on other camps supported by the main base at Cassinga and located around Chetequera.)

Back on the scene the two pilots – Commandant Ollie Holmes and Major Gerrie Radloff – spotted the convoy with the lead vehicles by then only a few kilometres south of the town. Holmes led and launched into an immediate high-angle strafing attack on the vanguard of the convoy, noticing as he did that three vehicles had already passed a bend in the road and had slipped out of his line of sight. These he delegated to Radloff who dealt with them promptly and effectively.

A brief orbit confirmed that the convoy had been halted and, reaching critical fuel levels, the two Mirage IIIs set a return course for AFB Ondangwa.

No sooner had they left the scene than the helicopter force loading men, equipment and casualties came under threat from two enemy tanks that appeared unexpectedly very close to the scene. The tanks were repeatedly attacked by a Buccaneer piloted by Captain Dries Marais who, even after exhausting his ammunition, buzzed the targets at low level to deflect them from the frantic activity underway around the helicopters. With moments to spare the last helicopter lifted into the air and made for home.

The SADF suffered three killed and eleven wounded while helicopter pilot Major John Church of 19 Squadron was awarded the Honoris Crux, a coveted South African military decoration, for his actions during the tense last few moment of the operation.

At its conclusion, Operation *Reindeer* was judged an unqualified success. Whatever other strategic objectives in terms of prospective captures may or may not have been achieved, PLAN had suffered a devastating setback to its operational capacity. However, while the tactical victory went to the SADF and the SAAF, the propaganda victory was wholly won by SWAPO. As was frequently the case in relation to both Rhodesian and South African external raids, claims that targeted facilities were innocent refugee camps occupied by women and children were consistently made, rather too consistently for it always to be true, but nonetheless no

This historic photo shows the four pilots and 12 ground crew of 2 Squadron who took part in Operation *Reindeer*.

Cobus Toerien in the gunner's seat of a Soviet-built ZPU-1 14.5mm heavy machine gun. Used in a ground role it had a maximum range of 2,000 metres. In an anti-aircraft role the range decreased to 1,400 metres. The optical sight can be seen in front of Cobus's head.

was no different and South Africa was vilified in the face of gales of moral outrage emanating from various international forums.

Be that as it may, international isolation was by then a fait accompli anyway and efforts underway internationally to begin the process of a negotiated settlement of the South West African issue were not in any way enhanced by what had taken place. SWAPO president Sam Nujoma had already made clear his intention of intensifying the armed struggle which the South Africans responded to in kind.

By the end of 1978, a landmark year for all involved, the all-important United Nations Security Council Resolution 435 – that proposing a ceasefire and United Nations-supervised elections in South African-controlled South West Africa – had been tabled and passed. This introduced the exhaustive on-again-off-again negotiation process that would accompany the war through its many chapters, and which would only succeed in winning South African approval in 1988 on the eve of the Eastern bloc collapse.

more than was ever required for it to be believed and reported internationally. There was little truth in these claims, although the villagization of larger and even smaller guerrilla camps tended to lead to an inevitable body count of women and children. Cassinga

CHAPTER FIVE:
THE SAAF IN RHODESIA

Early in 1979 12 Squadron SAAF was given the opportunity to take part in an interesting cooperation with the Rhodesian Air Force (RhAF) in the bombing of a ZIPRA base located some 1,000 kilometres from the Rhodesian border.[8]

This attack, codenamed Operation *Vanity*, was launched as a reprisal against the shooting down of an Air Rhodesia scheduled flight between Kariba and Salisbury with the loss of 59 passengers. This was the second such incident, the first occurring in September 1978 and resulting in the death of all but 18 passengers, ten of whom were later gunned down by a ZIPRA response team. White Rhodesia, needless to say, was outraged at both these incidences, neither of which, incidentally, registered any meaningful international protest. This tended to further impress upon the white populations of both Rhodesia and South Africa the profound public opinion shift that had taken place in

the few short decades since each had fought alongside the rest of the British family in two world wars.

The target was the Angolan railway town of Vila Luso located in central Angola. This was a highly ambitious attack requiring more long-range bomber capacity than the hard-pressed Rhodesians had available at the time. A request was made to the SAAF for the loan of three Canberras which took to the air from AFB Waterkloof on the evening of 25 February 1979, arriving at Victoria Falls a few hours later to a brief illumination of the airport lights before a strictly enforced blackout resumed. For the remainder of the evening a sortie plan was established before the crews turned in, in readiness for an early start.

The South African aircraft had already been armed with the standard alpha-bomb load of six mesh hoppers each containing 50 bombs. The Rhodesian aircraft were similarly primed with the addition of a payload of 1,000lb bombs, one of which, incidentally, failed to disengage from the aircraft and required making safe before being carefully removed on a bed of foam mattresses.

The strike leader for the operation was Squadron Leader Chris Dixon, a man famed for his calm and aplomb in the delivery of his famous 'Green Leader' speech to Zambian air traffic control during the Rhodesian attack on the Freedom Camp complex of Westlands Farm outside Lusaka in October 1978. Dixon had circled Lusaka Airport during the raid, warning air traffic control that any hostile action by the Zambian Air Force would be dealt with by the Rhodesians, even delaying the landing of a scheduled Kenya Airways flight until the operation was complete. No attempt was made by the Zambians to interfere and air traffic control complied with the Rhodesian request. During start-up Dixon's aircraft developed a radio fault and so lead was temporarily passed to Flight Lieutenant Ted Brent and his navigator Jim Russell. It is interesting to note the observation of Brigadier-General Dick Lord who recorded the episode in his book *From Fledgling to Eagle: The South African Air Force during the Border War*:

> Later that day, when Green Leader and his formation arrived at Fylde [airfield], the problem with Chris Dixon's radio was clearly identified. A length of electric wire had been duct-taped from the cockpit, through the crew's entrance door and along the fuselage to the radio bay at the back of the bomb bay, to replace a broken wire in one of the looms. Desperate measures by a desperate air force!

This was no doubt true but, despite it, the operation proceeded virtually without a hitch. Green Leader rejoined the formation over the Zambian town of Mongu on the Zambezi River and some 370 kilometres en route to the target. From there the formation climbed to 39,000 feet, accompanied by two RhAF Hunters armed with Sidewinder missiles as top cover, and continued on to the target. Shortly before arrival, the formation descended below cloud cover, entering a storm which cleared only minutes before the target came into view. "Bomb doors," came the calm order from Green Leader as the formation arrived overhead, smoothly flying through clear weather with very little activity evident on the ground and no incoming anti-aircraft fire. Bombs were successfully deployed, after which the formation smoothly turned in the direction of home and disappeared over the southern horizon, having encountered neither obstacle nor opposition from start to finish.

Initially, it had appeared as if the camp might have been deserted but an examination of film footage recorded by the South Africans' Vinten F95 camera revealed chaotic scenes on the ground in the midst of the drop that later concurred with the estimated death toll of a rather modest 160 killed and 500 wounded.

A pleasing epilogue to a highly successful raid was the shooting down of two Zambian Air Force Macchi aircraft by ZIPRA forces in a fit of the jitters.

For the next month or so the 12 Squadron Canberra fleet saw considerable action in support of a sequence of SADF raids into southern and central Angola from Owamboland and Caprivi, dealing with a number of known or suspected SWAPO bases. Operations *Rekstok* and *Saffran* included aerial bombardments of a number of targets in Angola and Zambia along with photo-reconnaissance flights by Mirage III RZs.

During the course of March 1979 a series of aerial raids was launched against targets inside Angola by Canberra bombers attacking targets in Muongo on 8 March in east–central Angola, followed later on the same day by Canberra attacks delivered against Vila Franca and Capindi, both east of the rail port of Lobito. The following day, 9 March, it was the turn of Henhombe, followed by Huambango, Henhombe again and Oshono. Attacks continued a few days later, on 14 March, this time targeting a large ANC training facility at Nova Catengue, situated some 40 kilometres south of Lobito, followed later on the same day by an attack against the settlement of Ediva, less that 100 kilometres into Angola in the southwest.

This incident has remained a curiosity in the history of the Border War. Immediately after the bomb release over Ediva, an aircraft piloted by Lieutenant Wally Marais was noticed to still have its bomb-bay doors open. Radio calls failed to elicit a response from either member of the crew. A companion aircraft manoeuvred close in and, although noticing no outward signs of damage to the aircraft, was able to determine that the pilot was slumped over the controls.

The stricken Canberra climbed slowly to 2,000 feet while decreasing speed, then, banking gently to port, decreased speed to about 200 knots before pitching violently upward, stalling and then plunging into the ground.

An intensive air search undertaken by two Mirage FICZs failed to locate the wreckage or to establish the cause of the crash or the fate of the crew. The moment that news of the loss of the Canberra became general the Angolans were quick to claim credit. Communiqués declared that six SAAF aircraft had been shot down during repeated bombing raids between 6 and 15 March, during which 132 tons of bombs had been dropped, killing 12 people and wounding thirty. The SADF made no effort to correct this misinformation other than to issue, through a spokesman, the comment that the Angolan communiqué contained "... certain delectable unthruths".[9] One such untruth must surely have been the death toll which would most certainly have exceeded a mere 12 fatalities.

Toward the end of 1979, meanwhile, the SAAF found itself frequently in the air over Zambia and Mozambique in support of Rhodesian cross-border raids. This was a critical year in the bitter and bloody war being fought north of the Limpopo as the beleaguered and depleted Rhodesian security forces increasingly sought to gain negotiation leverage by the relentless pummelling of guerrilla rear bases in Zambia and Mozambique and, moreover, to make the point to both host countries that aiding the enemies of Rhodesia would come at a mighty and unsustainable cost.

The first of these was Operation *Cucumber* which took place between 6 and 9 July and involved four SAAF Canberras accompanying RhAF Canberras on a low-level attack on a ZANLA base southeast of Cabora Bassa dam in the Tete Province of Mozambique.[10] Between 21 and 24 August 12 Squadron was again alongside RhAF Canberras, this time in an operation codenamed *Placid*, attacking ZIPRA targets in Zambia: four in Mulungusi, one in Rufunsa and two in Solwezi. The most iconic and memorable SAAF/RhAF combined operation, however, was Operation *Uric*, or *Bootlace* as it was codenamed in South Africa, which took place between 2 and 8 September 1979 and involved a comprehensive series of ground and air attacks on various targets along the Limpopo corridor running between the Mozambican capital of Maputo and the Rhodesian border at Malvernia/Vila Salazar.

Operation *Uric* was one of a series of hard-hitting, last-minute operations staged by the exhausted but unbroken Rhodesian security forces as a curtain-call to 90 years of proud military tradition, much of it undertaken in the company of the Springboks; certainly the involvement of the SAAF in this operation was a fitting valediction to a fading partner in arms. The operation required virtually every air asset the RhAF could put in the air and more besides. The Rhodesian commitment included eight aging Hawker Hunter strike jets, six Canberras, 12 C-47 Dakotas, six Cessna Lynx and 28 helicopters, mainly Alouette IIIs but also including a small flight of Bell 205s. The South African contribution amounted to 15 Pumas and two Super Frelons drawn from 19 and 15 squadrons respectively.

The operation involved a series of precision airstrikes targeting primarily the rail and road bridges up the length of the Limpopo corridor, with engineers and members of the SAS attempting to demolish the substantial road and rail bridge over the Limpopo at Aldeia da Barragem adjacent to the town of Chirunduo. An RhAF Bell 205 was lost during this action with a Rhodesian flight engineer killed and, although the bridge was seriously damaged, it was not destroyed. The operation also witnessed the loss of a South African Puma that was brought down by an RPG-7 rocket fired from the ground. The missile impacted the helicopter immediately behind the pilot, causing a violent roll to the right before the ship crashed into the ground in a ball of flame. Killed were Captain Paul Denzel Velleman, co-pilot Lieutenant Nigel David Osborne and flight engineer Sergeant Dirk Wilhelmus Marthinus (Dick) Retief. None of the 14 Rhodesian soldiers on board survived. The moment marked the single-worst loss of life sustained in combat by the Rhodesian security forces since the onset of the war. Two South African Puma pilots were decorated for valour after the battle: Commandant Breytenbach was awarded the Honoris Crux (Sliver) and Major Stannard the Honoris Crux.

Bootlace was followed soon afterward by Operation *Miracle*, another Rhodesian external raid, this time targeting a widely dispersed ZANLA base close to the Mozambican town of Chimoio. To this operation the SAAF contributed two Canberras. In late October, the last collaboration with the RhAF was

Commandant Breytenbach (left) chats with Air Marshal Frank Mussell (RhAF) in front of his SAAF Puma. Breytenbach was awarded an Honoris Crux (Sliver) for his actions during Operation *Bootlace/Uric*.

Puma 164, shot down over Mapai during Operation *Bootlace/Uric*.

Operation *Bootlace/Uric*: SAAF Pumas and Super Frelons in Mozambique. An RhAF Bell 205 is at right.

Operation *Tepid*, a major airstrike on a ZIPRA camp situated midway between Kariba and Lusaka. Again, it was the SAAF Canberras that took part.

By the end of 1979, the war in Rhodesia was effectively over and within a few months the curtain was drawn on the brief but dramatic history of this, the last problem child of the British Empire. Rhodesia became Zimbabwe and Zimbabwe became a new member of the OAU and the Front Line States, while South Africa inherited yet another hostile black African country

Mirage IIICZ, No 814, code letter red 0, No 2 Squadron, Port Elizabeth, on 18 June 1966 in the delivery scheme of Natural Metal and Red

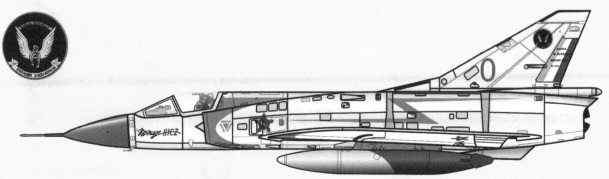

Red nose is a weighted substitute for the nose with the radar.

Mirage IIICZ, No 814, No 2 Squadron, used in the attack on Cassinga base, May 1978, Olive Drab and Deep Buff camouflage

CZ Serials: 800 – 815

Mirage III D2Z, No 845, 85 Combat Flying School, AFB Pietersburg, 1982

Mirage III D2Z, No 843, 85 Combat Flying School, Pietersburg, 1982

D2Z Serials: 843 – 853

Not to Scale

© W.S. Marshall - 2012

Mirage IIRZ, No 835, No 2 Squadron, AFB Waterkloof, Pretoria, in the delivery scheme of French Grey/Olive Green, 1970

RZ Serials: 835–838

Mirage IIRZ, No 835, No 2 Squadron, Waterkloof, Pretoria, in the bush war camouflage, late 1980s

Mirage IIIR2Z, No 854, No 2 Squadron, AFB Mpacha, SWA - recce mission to southern Angola, 1978

R2Z Serials: 854–857

Mirage IIIR2Z, No 855, No 2 Squadron, AFB Ondangwa, SWA, 1978

Not to Scale

© W.S. Marshall - 2012

Mirage F1CZ, No 206, No 3 Squadron, Capt A. Piercy was hit by AA-8 in a dogfight with MiG-23s, AFB Rundu, 1988

CZ Serials: 200 –215

Mirage F1CZ, No 203, No 3 Squadron, first MiG-21 kill by Maj J. Rankin, 6 Nov 1981

Mirage F1CZ, No 203, No 3 Squadron, Maj J. Rankin's second MiG kill, named 'Le Spectre', first F1 with the new low-viz scheme, 5 Oct 1982

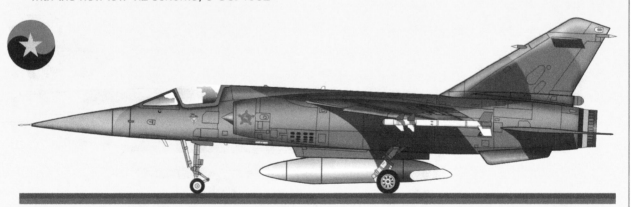

Mirage F1CZ, No 211, No 3 Squadron, armed with two Matra R550 missiles, AFB Ondangwa, 1984

Not to Scale

©W.S. Marshall - 2012

Mirage F1AZ, No 223, No 1 Squadron, with four 68mm Matra pods, Ondangwa, SWA, 1980

AZ Serials: 216 – 247

Mirage F1AZ, No 230, No 1 Squadron, with eight Mk 82 (250kg) bombs, Ondangwa, SWA, 1980

Mirage F1AZ, No 233, No 1 Squadron, with eight Mk 82 (250kg) bombs, Ondangwa, SWA, 1980

Mirage F1AZ, No 228, No 1 Squadron, with ferry tanks, en route to the operational area, SWA, 1980

Not to Scale

© W.S. Marshall - 2012

Buccaneer, No 423, No 24 Squadron, camouflaged in Dark Sea Grey and PRU Blue, Grootfontein, SWA, 1979

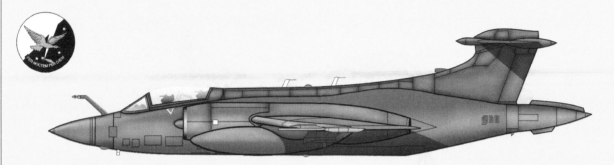

Canberra, No 452, No 12 Squadron, was shot down during Operation Rekstok on 14 March 1979

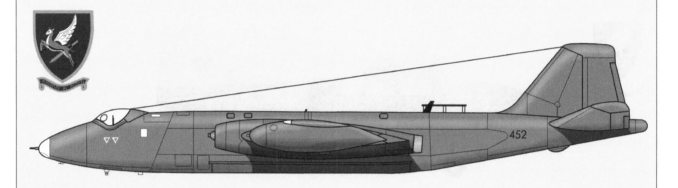

Impala Mk II, No 4 Squadron, Mapacha, in Olive and Deep Buff experimental camouflage scheme, fitted with six Matra F2 68mm pods, 1978

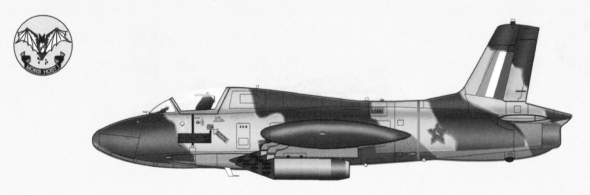

Impala Mk II, No 1057, No 4 Squadron, in the camouflaged scheme finally adopted, 1979

Not to Scale

©W.S. Marshall - 2012

Atlas AM3C Bosbok, No 920, flown by Capt D. Laubchser, armed with two Matra F2 68mm rocket pods firing smoke rockets with which he destroyed an AA site during Operation Protea, 1981

Cessna 185, No 737, No 11 Squadron, seen flying over Angola during Operation Savannah, 1976

Altas C4M Kudu, No 970, 41 Squadron, seen flying over the Ruacana area, 1979

Harvard II, No 7729, Central Flying School, in camouflage during deployment to the operational area, Grootfontein, Operation Savannah, 1976

Not to Scale

© W.S. Marshall - 2012

C-47 Dakota, No 6855, 44 Squadron, was hit by a SAM-7 missile southeast of Ondangwa but managed to make a safe landing there, 1986

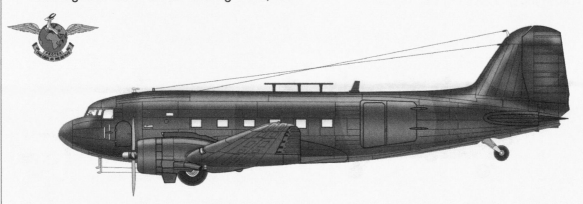

DC-4 Skymaster, No 44 Squadron, used for electronic surveillance in southern Angola while based at Grootfontein, SWA

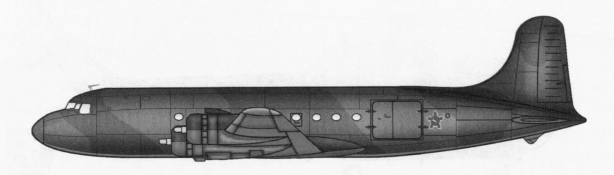

C-160 Transall, No 333, No 28 Squadron, used to drop paratroops during Operation Reindeer in May 1978

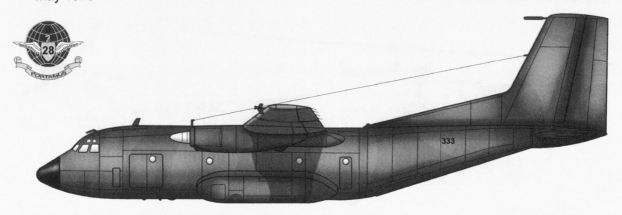

C-130 Hercules, No 403, No 28 Squadron, use for parachute drops and resupply missions in southern Angola, 1980s

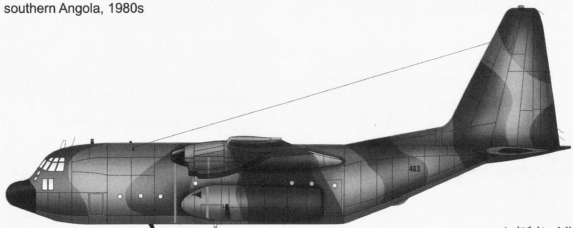

Not to Scale

© W.S. Marshall - 2012

SA 316 Alouette III, No 17 Squadron, during deployment in Angola, later used as a gunship armed with Browning and 20mm guns, 1980

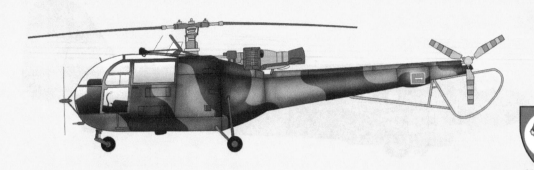

SA 330 Puma, No 130 from 19 Squadron, still in the early delivery scheme of French Olive Green, they were soon repainted in camouflage, Pretoria, late 1960s

SA 330 Puma, No 170 from No 19 Squadron, flown in the west of Owamboland on operations to support Himba tribesmen, 1980

SA-321L Super Frelon, from No 15 Squadron, was used to cargo-sling a recovered Cessna 185 which had crashed in Angola, 1978

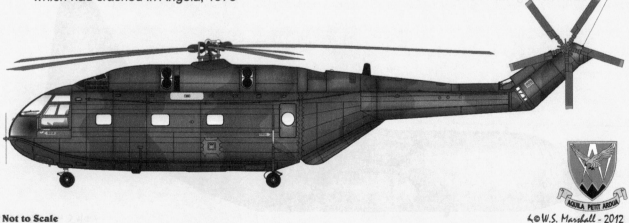

© W.S. Marshall - 2012

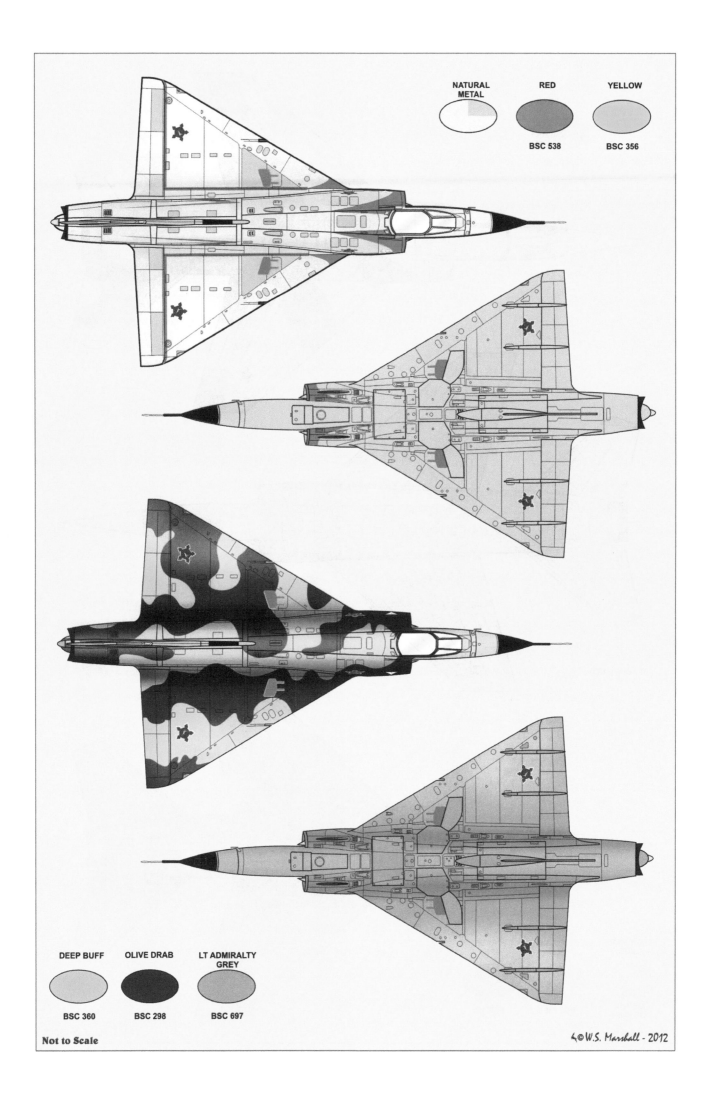

NATURAL METAL

RED

YELLOW

BSC 538

BSC 356

DEEP BUFF

OLIVE DRAB

LT ADMIRALTY GREY

BSC 360

BSC 298

BSC 697

Not to Scale

© W.S. Marshall - 2012

DEEP BUFF

BSC 360

OLIVE DRAB

BSC 298

LT ADMIRALTY GREY

BSC 697

HIGHVELDT GREY

BS 2660
BS 9-094

PRU BLUE

BSC 636

MIRAGE GREY

BSC 938

Not to Scale

©W.S. Marshall - 2012

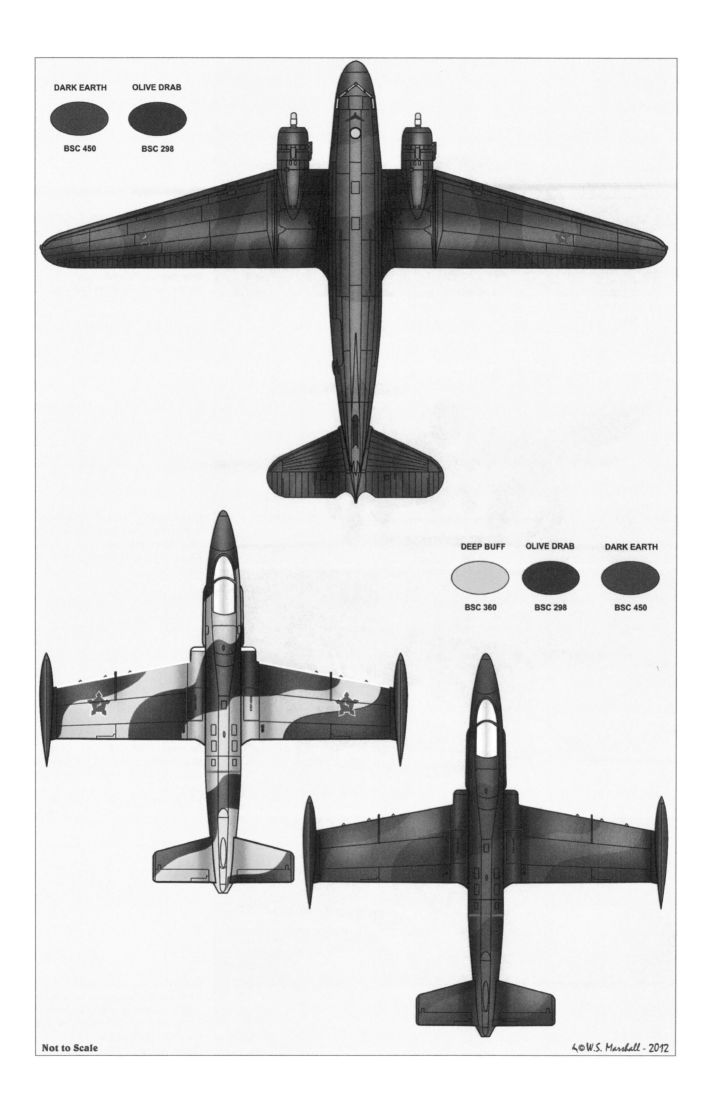

DARK EARTH   OLIVE DRAB

BSC 450   BSC 298

DEEP BUFF   OLIVE DRAB   DARK EARTH

BSC 360   BSC 298   BSC 450

Not to Scale

©W.S. Marshall - 2012

Alouette III, serial 629, with the emblem of 87 Helicopter Flying School, on the ramp at AFB Bloemspruit, Bloemfontein.
Photo courtesy William Marshall

Buccaneer S. Mk 50, 24 Squadron, Waterkloof, gloss Dark Sea Grey and PRU Blue undersides.
Photo courtesy William Marshall

Aermacchi AM.3C Bosbok, serial 595, painted in overall Light Grey, later camouflaged in Dark Earth and Dark Green.
Photo courtesy William Marshall

C160BZ Hercules, serial 405, in typical bush war colours, with few markings other than the required safety markings and single fuselage National Castle emblems.
Photo courtesy William Marshall

EE Canberra T. Mk IV, serial 458,
one of the SAAF's training aircraft,
on the apron at AFB Waterkloof
during the 1980s, painted in
overall PRU Blue.
Photo courtesy William Marshall

Douglas DC-4, in the bush war
colours of Dark Earth and Dark
Green with Azure Blue under
surfaces, no topside national
markings. Note the faded control
surfaces, a good example of
why these colours were used in
southern Africa.
Photo courtesy William Marshall

EE Canberra T Mk IV, serial 458,
in the earlier Silver, Black and
Dayglo colours, early 1970s.
Photo courtesy William Marshall

Cessna C-185, serial 730, in
natural metal.
Photo courtesy William Marshall

NA Harvard, serial 7475, in the SAAF's official training scheme of Silver and Dayglo. *Photo courtesy William Marshall*

NA Harvard camouflaged in Dark Earth and Dark Green, used during the 1975/6 period of Operation *Savannah* in Angola. These aircraft appeared in a variety of different patterns.
Photo courtesy William Marshall

Aermacchi MB326 Impala Mk II, serial 1012, in an interesting scheme of Deep Buff and Olive Drab where the Deep Buff is the dominant colour, later replaced by Dark Earth; white undersides with the interior of the wheel wells in Light Admiralty Grey.
Photo courtesy William Marshall

Aermacchi MB326 Impala Mk II, serial 1066, in Dark Earth and Dark Green, Light Admiralty Grey under surfaces with Red/Yellow safety markings. This was the final scheme these aircraft flew in until retirement. Note the power burn marks from the machine gun on the forward fuselage.
Photo courtesy William Marshall

Atlas C-4M Kudu, serial 970, 41 Squadron, in overall Dark Earth and Dark Green wraparound camouflage.
Photo courtesy William Marshall

Mirage IIIEZ, serial 842, gloss Buff and Dark Green top surface camouflage with Light Admiralty Grey under surfaces, Silver and Black nose cone. This aircraft was later converted to a Cheetah.
Photo courtesy William Marshall

Mirage IIIBZ, 2 Squadron, serial 816, possibly from the late 1960s, in the Silver and Red delivery colours with a Black nose cone; 2 Squadron emblem on the tail fin.
Photo courtesy William Marshall

Mirage F1AZ, 1 Squadron, serial 235, camouflaged in Dark Earth and Dark Green with the under surfaces in Light Admiralty Grey. This was the only aircraft in these experimental colours.
Photo courtesy William Marshall

Mirage F1CZ, 3 Squadron, serial 208, semi-gloss Buff and Dark Green top surface camouflage with the under surfaces in Light Admiralty Grey.
Photo courtesy William Marshall

Mirage F1CZ, 3 Squadron, serial 208, semi-gloss Buff and Dark Green top surface camouflage with the under surfaces in Light Admiralty Grey.
Photo courtesy William Marshall

Mirage IIID2Z, 85 Combat Flying School, serial 844, gloss Buff and Dark Green top surface camouflage with the under surfaces in Light Admiralty Grey.
Photo courtesy William Marshall

Aerospatiale, SA330 Puma, 19 Squadron, Swartkop, camouflaged in Dark Earth and Dark Green with polished air intakes.
Photo courtesy William Marshall

Aerospatiale, SA326 Super Frelon, 15 Squadron, camouflaged in Dark Earth and Dark Green.
Photo courtesy William Marshall

Operation *Bootlace/Uric*: A stick of Rhodesian SAS troops pose in front of a SAAF Puma.

Operation *Bootlace/Uric*: Rhodesian troops in front of a SAAF Super Frelon.

committed to her destruction. Political focus now shifted to South West Africa, and the independence agenda for a territory that the United Nations now officially referred to as Namibia.

South West Africa had initially been legally governed by South Africa as a League of Nations mandate which continued to be the case beyond the Second World War, notwithstanding gentle pressure from the League for South Africa to not grow too attached to the territory. Pretoria had indeed begun to regard South West Africa as a fifth province of the Union, making no secret of the fact that this was precisely how she would like to see the matter of future sovereignty resolved.

However, in 1966, the UN General Assembly passed Resolution 2145 that both terminated South Africa's mandate over South West Africa and assumed responsibility for the territory itself. A year later the Council for Namibia was formed with a view to mapping out a route toward independence in keeping with the general handover of power to indigenous responsibility that was underway continent-wide. South Africa ignored all this, continuing instead to integrate South West Africa into the South African political system, complete with a blueprint for the establishment of South African-style *bantustans* (black 'homelands').

Throughout the 1960s and 1970s the UN worked hard to pry South West Africa loose from South African control. World opinion, certainly where it mattered most, tended to be ambivalent at best. South Africa remained open for business, and business was good. South Africa, it must be remembered, occupied an economic stratum that bore almost no resemblance to any other on the continent. The SAAF, just as one example, was flying Mirage FIs, not one of which had been paid for by donor funds and nor were any current military assets gifts from a friendly government. South Africa was solvent and it had influence.

The 1980s, on the other hand, was very different. The international organization of the anti-apartheid movement had developed considerably, with placements in every major world capital, with ambassadors at large such as Winnie Mandela and Desmond Tutu and with such icons of the struggle as Steve Biko and Nelson Mandela to call on, an era of powerful and popular grassroot global support for change in South Africa was introduced. Most importantly though, South Africa found herself strategically alone and backed into a corner. In September 1978, United Nations Security Council Resolution 435 was adopted that proposed a ceasefire and UN-supervised elections in South African-controlled South West Africa, which ultimately was to lead to the independence of Namibia, nullifying any efforts South Africa was attempting to make to develop an internal settlement with moderate black interests that did not include SWAPO.

Throughout the remainder of the life of the Cold War, South Africa resisted ongoing and intensifying United Nations pressure for an inclusive settlement, stating consistently, and not altogether unreasonably, that an unopposed SWAPO walk-in and the unashamedly Marxist-oriented administration of Namibia that would undoubtedly occur was unacceptable to South Africa. This would remain the position until the collapse of the Soviet Union, at the end of the 1980s, removed the basis of this argument.

In the meanwhile, the war went on. The pattern of attrition aimed at preventing PLAN build-ups within striking distance of the cut-line and the running to ground and liquidation of those units that had succeeded in penetrating the country had gradually begun to take the sting out of SWAPO.

In addition, South Africa had become more deeply involved in supporting UNITA which had emerged from a point of virtual extinction in the late 1970s to a robust guerrilla organization with expanded relations with both the US and South Africa. Many of the key actions and operations that would define the 1980s on the battlefield were undertaken in cooperation with, or in support of, UNITA.

CHAPTER SIX:
OPERATIONS *PROTEA* AND *DAISY*, AND A TURNING OF THE TIDE

In an effort to shield itself from the unrelenting attentions of the SADF, PLAN had adopted the rather sensible strategy of nestling itself under the wing of FAPLA in the hope and understanding that South Africa, bearing in mind the ongoing political process and the general hue and cry that accompanied any overtly aggressive action, would baulk at mounting any direct action against the constituted armed forces of Angola. Several key SWAPO bases and command-and-control structures were therefore co-located alongside brigade-strength Angolan positions centred on the two southern Angolan towns of Xangongo and Ongiva. Both these were reasonably substantial towns, the latter located closer to the South West African border, no more than 50 kilometres from the Oshikango border post and within reasonably easy striking distance of SWAPO's designated 'North-western Front', the populous Owamboland native-autonomous area where SWAPO enjoyed most of its grassroot support, and the adjacent and considerably more remote Kaokoland, both located in SADF Sector 10 operational area. Surrounding both was a number of satellite camps and radar installations, all increasingly fortified by heavy weapons and strong anti-aircraft installations.

All this obviously presented a tempting target to the SADF which continued to exhaust manpower and equipment dealing piecemeal with an escalating SWAPO insurgency in the central border regions. In addition to this, such an obvious military build-up so close to the border, particularly in the matter of radar and anti-aircraft capability, represented an unacceptable level of threat to both border security and local air superiority.

As the South Africans pondered this rather brazen conventional build-up, a broader strategy began to evolve of clearing a buffer zone a minimum of 50 kilometres deep inside Angola, but practically speaking much deeper than this in places, to drive both FAPLA and PLAN north and away from a situation of being able to directly threaten South West Africa. This buffer zone would be known as the Shallow Area and could be justified as legal in the face of the inevitable hue and cry that would follow based on international laws which prohibit host countries, in this case Angola, from allowing surrogate organizations to launch hostile insurgencies from their territories into those of international neighbours.

Planning for Operation *Protea* began early in 1981. The objective would be to deal with the current military threat using a classic combined air and ground assault on two key installations, Xangongo and Ongiva, with further and very heavy air attention applied against various other related targets in order to knock out local radar coverage and the associated anti-aircraft emplacements. The main attack force would consist of two mechanized armoured

fighting groups, task forces Alpha and Bravo. TF Alpha, equipped with armoured cars, artillery, Ratel and Buffel armoured personnel-carriers, would handle the main assaults against Xangongo and Ongiva while TF Bravo would range farther afield in a search of known or suspected SWAPO training and logistics bases. Attached to each fighting group would be SAAF MAOTs, or mobile air operations teams, charged with liaison and advising on air support as the attack progressed.[11]

The air operation was to have a somewhat broader objective. Separately codenamed Operation *Konyn*, the SAAF was tasked, in addition to providing close air support to ground forces engaged in Operation *Protea*, with the disruption and destruction of Angolan air force and SWAPO air-defence systems in the central theatre by means of airstrikes targeting specifically the radar installations at two points, Chibemba and Cahama, both situated northwest of Xangongo. This was in addition to the usual interdiction, paratroop deployment, Telstar, casevac, air reconnaissance and target-spotting activities required in an operation of this size. In fact, the air operation would be the largest mounted by the SAAF since the Second World War, requiring a significant allocation of assets for the duration.

Operation *Protea* was scheduled to begin on 24 August 1981 but the SAAF were in the air several days prior to this, undertaking the usual interdiction missions alongside routine road- and photo-reconnaissance missions to update current intelligence prior to the launch. The first aircraft earmarked for the operation began to arrive at their border bases on 21 August. Clearly, there would be too many aircraft in operation to be deployed from a single facility, which required the Canberras of 12 Squadron, the Buccaneers of 24 Squadron and the Mirage F1AZs of 1 Squadron to be deployed to AFB Grootfontein, while the fighters of 2 and 3 squadrons and all the Impala light-attack jet aircraft were deployed to AFB Ondangwa. Various orientation exercises were undertaken in the days leading up to the operation, in particular for the attack aircraft which would be confronting established anti-aircraft artillery and shoulder-fired SA-7 Strela surface-to-air missiles.

On August 23, the day prior to the launch of the ground operation, air operations began in earnest. A four-ship Buccaneer strike was initiated against the radar installations at Cahama, using AS-30 guided missiles, which opened what would be a comprehensive and sustained mauling of these two key targets throughout the operation.[12] The Buccaneers were followed by a Canberra/F1CZ configuration in two waves, launching long-delay and contact-fused 250kg and 450kg bombs with little or no responding AAA ground fire.

At more or less the same time the Buccaneers went to work

Operation *Protea*: SADF briefing prior to the assault, with rows of Ratels in the background. *Photo courtesy Cameron Blake*

SADF task force stand by for the assault.
Photo courtesy Cameron Blake

SADF task force in readiness for the assault.
Photo courtesy Cameron Blake

An SADF Buffel rolls into action. *Photo courtesy Cameron Blake*

on the Chibemba installations, registering an SA-7 launch that detonated at 18,500 feet but did not compromise any of the attacking aircraft. Again, this was followed by composite waves of Canberra and Mirage aircraft using a level-bombing delivery technique to unload the same payload as upon Cahama. However, a release error resulted in the bulk of this ordnance being scattered about the surrounding bush. Later the same afternoon, a 16-ship Mirage F1 force revisited the target, recording a second SA-7 launch that, once again, missed its target. As the day closed and evening arrived, the attacks continued with additional Canberra and Buccaneer runs to further reinforce the pummelling of the

two key targets. At 20h30, well after dark, the day's activity was rounded off by a close air support mission flown by two Impalas in aid of a company of 31 Battalion pinned down by an aggressive SWAPO/FAPLA force.

The following day, 24 August, the main thrust of the operation was launched, with the SAAF focus now shifting to air support. A mechanized force very quickly established itself at Humbe on the opposite bank of the Cunene River from Xangongo and on the main highway north where it dug in to block any possible relief effort coming and also any effort on the part of beleaguered elements within Xangongo to attempt a breakout.

In the meanwhile, a second mechanized force crossed the border north of Ondangwa and made directly for Xangongo, detaching elements to isolate the target from a FAPLA force located at nearby Peu Peu, and to clean up satellite camps situated on the outskirts of Xangongo. The SAAF, meanwhile, directed sustained attacks on enemy positions in Humbe and Peu Peu as well as strongpoints, pockets of resistance and strategic targets within Xangongo itself.

Heavy anti-aircraft fire was registered against all attacking aircraft but by the end of day not one of the ground-operation aircraft had been lost. A Bosbok pilot, Captain Daan Laubscher, was later awarded the Honoris Crux for taking out a 23mm gun position that had stalled a troop advance, flying into intense AAA fire as he attacked the target with 68mm SNEB rockets.

August 25, D-Day + 1, was not so auspicious. As TF Alpha spent the day consolidating its position in the now-occupied town of Xangongo, an Alouette III was brought down with 23mm AAA fire near Mongua. In the meanwhile, TF Bravo had succeeded in capturing the small town of Ionde, northeast of Xangongo, which boasted a sand airstrip, increasing SAAF flexibility significantly and allowing for logistical resupply to the ground forces operating in the area as well as prompt casualty evacuation.

With Xangongo secured the focus of the ground operation then shifted to Ongiva, the administrative capital of Cunene Province. A combined FAPLA/SWAPO attempt to halt the mobile SADF force at Mongua was brushed aside before the South Africans set upon the dug-in defences of the town in earnest, securing first the airport, which was the first target approached by road, and then moving on the town proper.

The SAAF was in the thick of the battle throughout, attacking military installations and AAA sites surrounding the town and the airfield. A Strela hit on a Mirage III piloted by Captain Rynier Keet was recorded during a strike aimed at the Ongiva airport. The impact occurred at the top of the tailpipe section and, although severely debilitated, Keet was able to return to base and put the ship down, having been ordered to orbit until all other aircraft had landed to avoid the possibility of a stricken aircraft obstructing the runway.

Close air support operations continued as TF Alpha methodically worked its way through the expansive target area, calling in air assaults on tank, mortar and 122mm rocket positions which from time to time stalled the advance. A particular obstacle frequently encountered was dug-in armoured vehicles and tanks where only the turret was protruding and which were being used as static artillery. These were very difficult to take out as the vulnerable wheels and tracks were protected by sand revetments.

At about 15h00 a large convoy of enemy vehicles was seen attempting to break out of the town heading northeast on the main highway leading to Menongue. This was rather a desperate gambit bearing in mind the swarm of lethal SAAF aircraft buzzing the scene and, needless to say, it was not long before it ran into and was halted by a TF Bravo stop group, leaving it static and highly vulnerable on a clearly defined road. Two Mirages were called in to attack the ostensibly free-gift target but found the head of the column and the stop group too close to each other to risk firing. This offered an opportunity to a number of vehicles to peel off into the dense bush surrounding the road and attempt an escape around the enemy flank. These, however, were pursed by a Bosbok and quickly located, after which a pair of Impalas was called in to deal with them. Once these had expended their ordnance, four Alouette gunships took over, relieved later by another unit of three Alouette gunships. During this brief but joyous action the SAAF accounted for 13 vehicles while skirmishing ground forces took out another three. These included T-34 tanks and several Soviet BTR armoured personnel-carriers. It was noted that among the

SADF troops awaiting the conclusion of the aerial bombardment of Ongiva prior to the assault. *Photo courtesy Cameron Blake.*

A Puma disgorges assault troops. *Photo courtesy Cameron Blake.*

A wounded capture is led away toward an awaiting Puma. *Photo courtesy Cameron Blake.*

Operation *Protea*: a casevac being transferred from a field ambulance to a Puma arriving in a cloud of dust. *Photo courtesy Cameron Blake.*

A captured FAPLA soldier is guided to an awaiting Ratel.
Photo courtesy Cameron Blake.

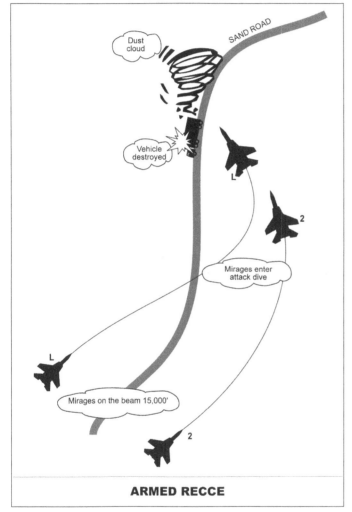

for either SWAPO or FAPLA to operate effectively within the Shallow Area. Most important was the fact that both locations were equipped with serviceable airfields that were improved by SAAF airfield maintenance crews, after which they were available for use, mainly by transport aircraft, but also, when necessary, by helicopters and other ground-support aircraft.

The last SAAF missions flown in support of ground forces were on 28 August, with attacks and general activity also underway in the TF Bravo area of operations, most amounting to little because the SWAPO presence in this sector had rapidly evaporated upon the launch of the general action. It hardly mattered however, since, with the main logistical nerve centres incised, there would be nothing around which hostile forces could coalesce. In fact, it was noted in the months that followed the operation that most encounters with SWAPO tended to be with disconnected groups concerned more with simple survival than offensive operations.

By 1 September, the last withdrawing South African infantryman had crossed the border, returning to South West Africa with considerable booty, amounting, according to Border War historian Willem Steenkamp, to some 2,000 tonnes of looted ammunition, anti-aircraft guns, vehicles ranging from lorries and recovery tractors to scout cars and tanks and many other items.[13]

The net result of the operation was that both SWAPO and FAPLA were pushed northward, with the ability of SWAPO to easily access South West African territory reduced by both distance and, at least temporarily, the destruction or removal of their main heavy weapons inventory. This was grounds for brief elation as the operation wound down and the tactically superior South African forces justly congratulated themselves on a job well done. However, the fact remained that a comprehensive rearming by both FAPLA and SWAPO would be delayed simply by the practicalities of expediting another series of shipments from Russia, all of which would be of the latest pattern and, of course, a sharp improvement on what had been there before.

However, as things stood, the international furore welled, peaked and broke with little material change to the moribund political process and with, underlying it all, an unmistakable note of respect for the fact that South Africa had again proved her considerable tactical superiority on the battlefield. For the loss of ten SADF soldiers and two SAAF personnel, over 1,000 combined enemy deaths had been reported, a massive haul of enemy matériel accrued and a gain of enemy territory – although the latter was fervently denied – that included Xangongo and Ongiva, both of which remained under South African occupation for quite some time.

The Angolans, meanwhile, fulminating with understandable gusto in all the international forums available, had been forced to swallow being chased out of a significant swath of their own country, with no serious attempt made by the local air force, notwithstanding generous donations of Soviet aerial hardware, to challenge South African domination of the skies. For the South Africans, it was without doubt a satisfying way to end an impressive military operation.

dead were four Russians – two men and two women – while a Soviet sergeant-major was captured. What became of him has never been explicitly revealed but it can be taken for granted that he was used in some way as proof that the whole war was premised on South Africa deflecting Soviet expansionism in Africa.

Ongiva, meanwhile, was taken after a two-day battle. Thereafter, a strong SADF force remained in effective occupation of both Xangongo and Ongiva where they would remain on rotation for some time. The South African occupation of these two key administrative centres, notwithstanding being a constant stone in the shoe of any effort to broker an agreement between the warring parties as the political process continued, made it impossible

Enemy ordnance captured during Operation *Protea*.

However, no sooner had the dust settled over Xangongo and Ongiva than intelligence began to come to light of SWAPO efforts to regroup at its regional headquarters located at Chitequeta, some 150 kilometres inland and west of the SADF-occupied Xangongo/Ongiva complex. Operation *Daisy* was planned and launched, on 1 November 1981, as an SADF mechanized force crossed the border into Angola. A tactical HQ was established at Ionde, 120 kilometres inside Angola, with a SAAF MAOT and a HAA/HAG where forces were later assembled in readiness for the advance on Chitequeta.

Air activities began again on 4 November with six C-130 and C-160 transporters dropping three companies of paratroopers into the target area. Bosboks were airborne over the battle for most of the day, playing reconnaissance, target-spotting and Telstar roles as the mechanized force and paratroop companies went into action. Low-level bombing by the Buccaneer fleet followed soon afterward, accompanied by four Mirage F1AZs, and again followed a moment later by three F1CZs, each recording some retaliatory AAA fire and one SA-7 launch that failed to find its target.

Day two of the air operation followed a similar pattern, remarkable only for the explosion of an ammunition-laden Buffel armoured personnel-carrier at a forward HAG, forcing an evacuation of all helicopters located there. Day three, however, was a singularly remarkable day, both in terms of Operation *Daisy* in particular and the SAAF's Border War in general. On that day, despite being present at the edges of the action many times before and flying in a generally defensive posture, the Angolan MiGs, that hitherto largely unknown quantity, finally became aggressive.

In anticipation of something like this an aerie of Mirage F1CZs, armed with missiles and 30mm cannons, had at all times been standing at cockpit standby[14] in readiness shelters at AFB Ondangwa. At 07h00 two fast-moving tracks were detected on radar moving south from Lubango where a large Angolan airbase was located toward the town of Quiteve. Two F1CZs, piloted by Major Johan Rankin and with Lieutenant Johan du Plessis as his wingman, were quickly scrambled onto an intercept vector. Hoping to avoid a repeat of earlier retirements by Angolan MiGs at the moment that they detected an incoming interception, Rankin and du Plessis approached at low level up the Cunene River before bursting into full radar view at combat speed. Both pilots were graduates of the South African 85 Advanced Fighter School based at AFB Pietersburg and both had had been invested with extensive training in air combat manoeuvre (ACM) for precisely this eventuality.

It was du Plessis who first made visual contact with the enemy flying in the opposite direction between three and five miles away on the port beam. Both were identified as MiG-21s flying in a fighting element formation at the same altitude as the Mirages. Jettisoning their drop tanks the Mirages assumed a clean profile and entered a hard left turn, positioning themselves generally behind the unsuspecting MiGs. The two enemy aircraft were flying 1,000 to 1,500 feet distant from one another with the No. 2 aircraft trailing 30 degrees behind the leader's beam. They were also flying directly into the sun which tended to preclude a shot from the Mirages armed with Matra 550 heat-seeking missiles, so Rankin, closing from astern of the enemy, fired a burst of 30mm explosive shells from a distance of approximately 350 metres. The shots registered instantly on the now intensely alert MiG which immediately began to leak fuel from its fuselage.

Both MiGs then responded by entering a tight descending left-hand turn while at the same time jettisoning their external fuel tanks. Rankin, at this point within range of the lead MiG, attempted to launch a missile which malfunctioned. He then peeled off the lead MiG and entered a curve of pursuit on the second MiG, ordering du Plessis to hone in on the wounded leader. Rankin's new quarry then landed almost in his lap by committing a fundamental error of air combat, reversing his left-hand turn, which allowed the pursuing South African Mirage bearing in from the left to cut in directly behind him, from where, at close range, a burst of cannon fire exploded the hapless ship, breaking it up and forcing Rankin to violently shear away in order to avoid the debris. He glanced back

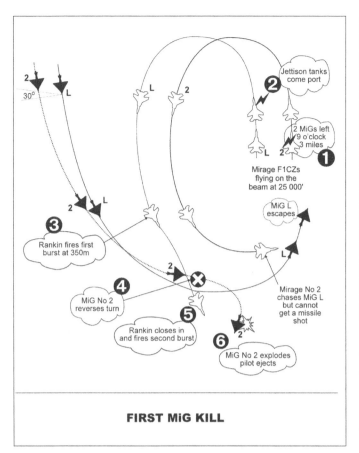

FIRST MiG KILL

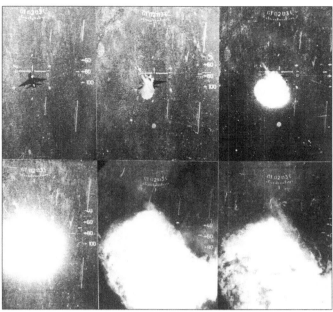

MiG-21 kill sequence as seen through Rankin's gun sight.

Johan Rankin (left) congratulated by Jack Gründling for shooting down the first MiG-21 of the war.

to see the MiG spiralling to the ground and, as every combat pilot wishes under similar circumstances, he observed the pilot eject.

Du Plessis, in the meanwhile, had followed the MiG leader as it entered into a desperate spiral manoeuvre and twice entered the Mirage's firing parameters but each time the Matra 550s malfunctioned, the high G descending turn possibly exceeding its launch limits. The fortunate MiG was able to make good its escape.

The moment was a sweet one at AFB Ondangwa as the victorious Mirages touched down. This was the first enemy aircraft shot down by the SAAF since the Korean War and certainly the first in the current conflict. It did, however, lead to considerable discussion regarding a shift in tactical approach by the Angolan fighter fleet and indeed the Angolan military in general, and what this might mean in terms of future encounters, particularly now that it had been revealed that the South African missiles could be relied upon to malfunction in crucial combat conditions.

It was clear now that the days of assumed air superiority by the South Africans on external operations was a thing no longer to be taken for granted.

CHAPTER SEVEN:
MIG HUNTERS AND MOONLIGHT OPERATIONS

With the actions and ramifications of operations *Protea* and *Daisy*, the Border War had clearly escalated to something approaching an undeclared conventional war with Angola. Likewise, the ongoing political process that had accompanied it all also sharply escalated, devolving very quickly into a multilateral squabble involving all the member states of both the United Nations and the Organization of African Unity, the Soviets and the Cubans and, of course, South Africa and the United States. On behalf of the former the baton was carried by South Africa's charismatic and

mercurial Minister of Foreign Affairs Pik Botha, and on behalf of the latter by the somewhat less charismatic but no less competent US Assistant Secretary of State for African Affairs Chester Crocker. In the months and years prior to this, a so-called UN Western Contact Group, which had comprised the US, Britain, France, West Germany and Canada, had sought to find a solution to what had in effect become a matter of global power play. With such overt Soviet and Cuban involvement in Angola and with the support offered SWAPO by each of these, South Africa could

The Buccaneer was perhaps the best aircraft in the SAAF arsenal in terms of an African war. It could fly fast and low over great distances while carrying 'everything plus the kitchen sink'.

The Mirage III was a wonderful fighter but limited fuel capacity restricted its use over the vast expanse of the combat area.

clearly not be expected to withdraw from the region in preparation for the multiparty elections in South West Africa proposed by UN Resolution 435, since no such thing would ever happen. Western interests, in particular US interests, would also not be served by a dominant Cuban–Soviet role in the process, and so when SWAPO called an end to the procedure, claiming bias toward South Africa on the part of the contact group, it could not be fairly stated that this was not so. The US position was revised under Ronald Reagan to include a link between a South African withdrawal from South West Africa with a Cuban troop withdrawal from Angola, which was of incalculable value to South Africa in the short term, but which also served to ensure that no meaningful progress could be made either. And there the matter rested.

In the meanwhile, the war went on. In the aftermath of operations *Protea* and *Daisy*, two key changes were observed in SWAPO's operational status. In terms of the local insurgency, it had been the pattern in the past for small groups, operating as much as possible under the South African radar, to enter the country under the platoon-level command of experienced cadres. It was noticed now that far larger groups of nominally trained fighters were making an appearance in the field, with a more thinly spread command element. This was interpreted as evidence

that many better trained and experienced members of PLAN had been removed from the scene by intense South African attrition. Secondly, it was becoming clear that SWAPO front-line manpower was increasingly being diverted away from activities on the border to help the MPLA deal with UNITA incursions, indicating, if nothing else, the extent to which UNITA had grown in reach capacity.

The latter point was extremely important in view of the gradual evolution of the Border War. UNITA would grow to occupy an increasingly important role both in terms of its alliance with South Africa and the extent to which this in the months and years to follow would draw South Africa deeper into the Angolan civil war proper.

In the meanwhile, the first major action of 1982 was Operation *Super*, a somewhat routine affair that grew out of a Special Force reconnaissance insertion into the southern Namibe Province of Angola in order to follow up on intelligence suggesting considerable SWAPO vehicle traffic in the area. The Recces alerted a SWAPO detachment to their presence by laying a vehicle landmine that detonated under the wheels of a passing armoured personnel-carrier. No SWAPO members were injured in the explosion but a follow-up was begun that quickly compromised the Recces, who called in reinforcements from the hard-fighting 32 Battalion. Thereafter, a brisk firefight was fought with the aid of a SAAF Alouette gunship fitted with a 20mm cannon. Once the dust had settled, 21 SWAPO guerrillas were dead, six were captured and one had escaped.

Interrogation of the captured guerrillas revealed a large and previously unknown SWAPO concentration in the rugged Cambêno Valley southeast of the Iona National Park. On 13 March 1982, a mobile Fire Force of 45 men of 32 Battalion, transported in a flotilla of SAAF Puma helicopters supported by Alouette gunships, set off across the dry expanse of the Kaokoveld toward a temporary base established in the Marienflüss Valley, with logistics supplied by a DC-3 Dakota.[15]

The infantrymen were dropped by Puma and succeeded in taking the camp in an action that extended over eight hours, supported continuously by Alouette gunships. The fight resulted in the deaths of 201 SWAPO members to the loss of three men of 32 Battalion. A new prospective infiltration route was also comprehensively shut down. Captain Ellis, who had coordinated the air assault from above, and Sergeant Stephen Coetzee were both awarded the Honoris Crux for their actions that day. Three members of 32 Battalion were similarly decorated.

1982 was a year of mixed fortunes for the SAAF. On 1 June an Impala Mk II, piloted by Major Gene Kotze, was successfully brought down by enemy anti-aircraft fire while diving to attack a SWAPO target inside Angola. The aircraft crashed, killing the pilot instantly. Then, two months later, on 9 August, a fully loaded Puma was brought down near Cassinga by either a direct hit from a ground-fired RPG-7 rocket or a 23mm AAA – reports on the matter differ – killing pilot Captain John Twaddle, co-pilot Lieutenant Chris Petersen, technician Sergeant Grobler and all 12 paratroopers on board.

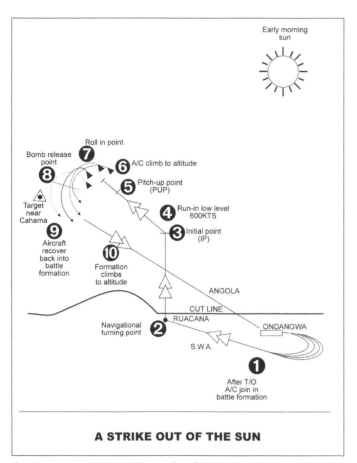

Early morning sun

7 Roll in point
6 A/C climb to altitude
Bomb release point **8**
5 Pitch-up point (PUP)
Target near Cahama
4 Run-in low level 600KTS
9 Aircraft recover back into battle formation
3 Initial point (IP)
10 Formation climbs to altitude

ANGOLA

CUT LINE
RUACANA
Navigational turning point **2**
ONDANGWA
S.W.A.

1
After T/O A/C join in battle formation

A STRIKE OUT OF THE SUN

On 16 May, eight Mirage AZs and four CZs destroyed enemy 23mm and 57mm AAA positions at Cahama, a constant thorn in the SAAF's side.

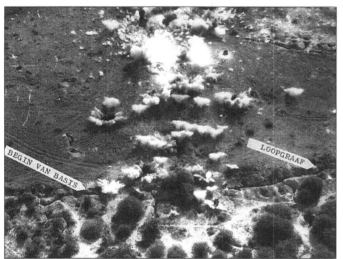

BEGIN VAN BASIS

LOOPGRAAF

Another strike on Cahama, this time by Canberras.

Armed Impala Mk II aircraft taxiing for take-off at AFB Ondangwa, 1982. *Photo: SAAF Museum*

Matters were put right, however, when 3 Squadron's Major Johan Rankin, this time flying with Captain Cobus Toerien as his wingman, successfully brought down another Angolan MiG-21 in aerial combat. On this occasion the F1CZs were tasked to escort an extremely vulnerable and very valuable Canberra on a small-area photo-reconnaissance mission over the Cahama area for the purpose of updating intelligence. At 11h20 the two fighters rendezvoused with the Canberra and, under positive radar control, the three-ship formation set a course for Cahama. Very quickly, however, radar fighter-control picked up approaching enemy aircraft and ordered the Canberra back while instructing the two fighters to climb to 30,000 feet and accelerate to Mach 0.95, the limiting speed for external fuel tanks. This positioned the opposing formations nose-to-nose, 12 nautical miles apart and closing at twice the speed of sound.

Major Rankin observed two MiG-21s on the same level as him, some five nautical miles distant, flashing past on his starboard side. The two F1 pilots shed their drop tanks, went into afterburner and commenced a hard right-hand turn in pursuit. Moments before the two formations crossed, the MiGs fired their missiles but they had no chance then of guiding correctly. In the meanwhile, the F1s completed their 180-degree turn as the MiGs were turning smoothly to the right, preserving their supersonic speed. Radar confirmed that they were inching ahead of the F1s and out of firing range. Unable to close, Rankin switched his intercept radar onto transmit in the hope that the MiG radar warning receiver would

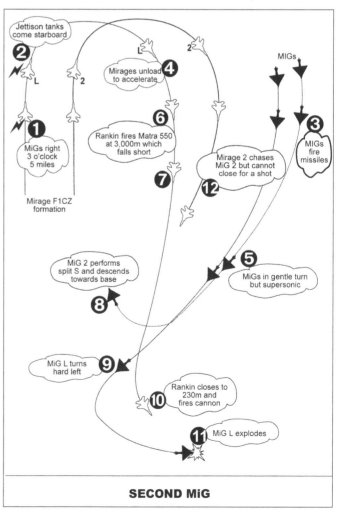

Jettison tanks come starboard **2**
L **4** Mirages unload to accelerate **2**
MIGs
1 MiGs right 3 o'clock 5 miles
6 Rankin fires Matra 550 at 3,000m which falls short
3 MiGs fire missiles
Mirage F1CZ formation
7
Mirage 2 chases MiG 2 but cannot close for a shot **12**
5 MiGs in gentle turn but supersonic
MiG 2 performs split S and descends towards base **8**
MiG L turns hard left **9**
Rankin closes to 230m and fires cannon **10**
11 MiG L explodes

SECOND MiG

Captain Cobus Toerien, Johan Rankin's wingman.

This close-up of the Shilka shows the operators in the turret, the four-barrelled 23mm cannons and the Gun Dish radar.

alert their pilots and force them to turn into the F1s. This was indeed what happened, whether as a result of the radar warning or simply because they were still focused on intercepting the Canberra, will never be known, but the sudden change of vector allowed the F1s to cut the corner and close the range.

The two South African fighters then performed an energy acceleration, reaching Mach 1.3 as they entered a curve of pursuit. Rankin made a snap estimation of range and, although his radar had not locked onto the target, he let loose a Matra 550 infrared missile which tracked the MiG until it reached all-burnt range before it fell away. Subsequent examination of the gun-camera footage revealed that the missile had been fired at 3,000 metres, the outer limit of its range at such speeds.

Continuing to close range, however, Rankin fired his second missile from a more practical range of 1,500 metres and this time the missile tracked the MiG which had begun a descending split-S manoeuvre, exploding right behind it.

The MiG was hit, and badly damaged, but still controllable. It slipped the net, continuing its left-hand roll before levelling out and running for home ahead of a trail of smoke. Later intelligence revealed that the damaged craft reached base but was unable to lower its undercarriage and was further damaged in a crash landing.

The remaining MiG, however, still had a fight on its hands and entered a split-S turn to the left with Rankin hard on its tail and overtaking rapidly. At a range of 200 metres the South African opened fire with his 30mm cannons, hitting the MiG which exploded directly in front of him, forcing the F1 through the expanding fireball which resulted in an engine compressor stall. Only after cutting the engine and performing a hot-relight was Rankin back in the game.

Brigadier-General Dick Lord, to whom the author owes thanks for his detailed account of this incident, makes an additional note that the aircraft Rankin was flying on this occasion was F1CZ 203, at that time the only aircraft in the SAAF arsenal painted in the

air superiority blue–grey colour scheme that was still at that point under evaluation but that would in due course appear on the other F1CZs of the SAAF.

At the same time as these exciting events were taking place, a more routine but nonetheless successful system of operations codenamed Operation *Maanskyn*, or *Moonshine*, was being put to good use over the Shallow Area. *Maanskyn* were specific night-flying operations that were scheduled to utilize the moonlight during the five nights prior to a full moon and for five nights subsequent. Visual armed reconnaissance flights using Impalas had quickly put a stop to the daytime movement of SWAPO logistics along the main roads in southern Angola, teaching the enemy to avoid travel during the day in recognition of the fact that the SAAF was known not to operate at night.

The reason for this was the deaths of two experienced Impala pilots in 1976 during a night-weaponry trial at the Reimvasmaak weapons range which resulted in the banning of the tactic ever since. Early in 1980, however, a series of specifically authorized night-flight sorties over the area immediately north of the cut-line had been conspicuously successful, reigniting interest in the idea and prompting a renewed series of experiments. A handful of simple innovations were developed in cooperation with specialists from the SAAF and Atlas Aviation that helped iron out some of the obvious problems associated with the highly sensory business of night flying.

The aircraft modified for this purpose were Impalas, dubbed the *Maanskyn* aircraft. The attitude indicator located in the centre of the instrument panel was the main source of reference required by a pilot to recover from an unusual position or extreme attitude. It was necessary that this vital instrument be isolated from the rest of cockpit illumination in order that other lights could be dimmed to protect the night vision of the pilot. This would allow the pilot to be alert to light activity on the ground with a clearly visible attitude indicator providing his primary reference for recovery after a dive attack.

SA-3 missiles being paraded through Luanda.

SAAF casevac.

Another innovation was an audio bomb-release device that allowed the pilot to dial in a bomb-release altitude for the weapons on board. As the pilot entered his dive attack, a low audio warning would commence at 1,800 feet before the release altitude, gathering in intensity at 500 feet above, until it cut off altogether at the precise required altitude. This allowed the pilot to apply all his attention on the approaching target without having to constantly cross-reference the altimeter.

The attack profile arrived at was the standard 30-degree dive angle used when firing 68mm rockets, in order to utilize a proven gun-sight setting. A secondary advantage of this shallow dive profile was that the height lost in recovery after release was not excessive. In addition to all this, all white lights in the crew room were replaced by red lights which helped in the quick achievement of good night vision which under normal circumstances can take up to an hour.

After a period of successful trials, the *Maanskyn* teams were deployed to AFB Ondangwa and let loose over the cut-line under the famous call sign Skunk. The patrol profile was relatively straightforward. Pilots would cruise at a low 200 KIAS (knots indicated air speed) with all armament switches selected to 'live' as they crossed into Angola. When the lights of a vehicle came into view the pilot then adjusted his offset position for the roll-in point, pulling his throttle to idle and silencing the undercarriage warning horn before rolling into the dive. Then it was simply a matter of tracking the target and waiting for the audio cues from the bomb-release altimeter before firing. A 37-degree angle was arrived at to achieve the correct release conditions, while, approaching the vehicle or convoy from the rear, a spot some 50 to 60 metres ahead on the moving vehicle was selected, more or less at the extremity of the headlight beam. The forward velocity of the vehicle reduced the dive angle to the required 30 degrees at release.

At the point of firing, the pilot would initiate the pull-out, concentrating solely on the illuminated attitude indicator. As the aircraft's nose rose through the horizon, dive brake in and full throttle were selected to quickly climb out of small-arms range. The pilots would circle when climbing back up to cruising altitude, vigilant at their six o'clock for any surface-to-air missile launches. The drill, should this happen, was to break into the approaching

missile and disengage back down to low altitude before heading for home.

A safe separation of between four to five miles between aircraft was maintained using the air-to-air mode of the Tacan (tactical airborne navigation) beacon. For additional safety a vertical separation of 2,000 feet was also maintained. All *Maanskyn* sorties were controlled by the mobile radar unit (MRU) and AFB Ondangwa.

Maanskyn operations quickly became a feature of the monthly peak-moon cycle, with the success of the strategy being clearly illustrated by the fact that vehicle traffic on the ground under full beam ceased, with just parking lights being used which, in the event, did nothing to ease the carnage since these were just as easily spotted in the blackness of the Angolan night. Flight times were varied to maintain as much of the surprise element as possible, focusing on three main lines of road communication existing in the Cunene Province: the Cahama–Xangongo blacktop road, the Mulondo–Quiteve sand road and the Cuvelai–Ongiva sand road.

Inevitably though, those needing to transit these routes at night recognized the correlation between the moon phases and SAAF air activity and simply avoided moonlit nights, moving during the dark phases at either end of the cycle. Thus *Maanskyn* operations began to include a *donkermaan*, or 'dark moon' variant, that simply required a little more training and a great deal more nerve. A greater reliance tended to be placed on aircraft separation using the Tacan air-to-air mode for the obvious fact that close formation in moonless conditions, with navigation lights extinguished, was both difficult and dangerous.

By the beginning of 1983, although night interdiction operations were being consistently flown, targets had become rare and kills even rarer. SWAPO and FAPLA had by then ceased nighttime travel altogether. In an attempt to diversify, it was decided from January onward that once a formation had reached the limit of its planned patrol, they would deliver their weapons on a selected target before returning to base. Obviously the selection of targets was carefully considered and made after extensive analysis of aerial photographic intelligence. According to Brigadier-General Dick Lord:

Within a few nights of this type of operation we started to reap unexpected benefits. On the first night, as the pinpoint target for the leader's rockets we had selected a newly built AAA site just outside Mulondo. The target area we chose for the shepherd [second aircraft] was an area of thick bush just west of Quiteve, the type loved by SWAPO.[16]

Regular radio intercepts revealed a certain amount of consternation in the enemy camp, with reports circulating of accurate attacks and victims such as 'the Russians'. Apart from adding to the general intelligence picture, this sort of feedback was very encouraging. A three-month plan was drawn up with a view to mounting one or two sorties a night with varying times and targets selected from known intelligence, or any suitable 'suspect' area.

The whole concept was extremely successful, so much so that the Angolans began to exert considerable pressure on the United States through the United Nations, which in turn translated into pressure on Pretoria, all of which filtered down to the ops room at Ondangwa.

The operation was ostensibly curtailed but mischief went on nonetheless. It must be remembered that the on-again-off-again negotiated process required that all sides at least *appear* to be playing the game fairly.

Dick Lord was, however, very impressed upon taking a road trip from Xangongo to Cahama, a 70-kilometre stretch of arterial road, by the sheer weight of destruction that *Maanskyn* and *Donkermaan* had wrought in the southern provinces. Every few kilometres or so there lay a cluster of wrecked tanks, military transports and troop carriers, in some cases blocking the road. To this day, a great deal of this detritus of war remains in slow decay along most of the byways of southern Angola, and in many other parts of the country too, lending irony once again to the fact that armed institutions such as the SADF and the SAAF, that failed at no point to achieve every military objective they sought, could still ultimately lose the war.

CHAPTER EIGHT:
ASSISTANCE TO UNITA AND OPERATION *ASKARI*

1983 opened on a stage of intense international diplomacy over the crisis. The sheer weight of international thought and effort being applied to the matter of ending the war in Angola and introducing some mutually acceptable roadmap toward Namibian independence seemed, at times, to be so much more than the sum total of its parts. Bilateral talks had been underway in Cape Verde since December and seemed, by January, to be yielding the possibility of a ceasefire based on a South African proposal that Cuban and other foreign troops be withdrawn to above the 14th parallel, about 150 kilometres north of the border. This, however, would have left the MPLA more or less unsupported against UNITA in the key southeast of the country. (UNITA was not party to the proposal.) The Angolans countered with the suggestion that a demilitarized zone 50 kilometres deep be created that would, by extension, have had to include UNITA for it to be effective. Rumours continued to circulate, generating some degree of cautious diplomatic optimism, but only some. In reality, the military option remained the most attractive to both sides, with each grappling for some definitive advantage on the battlefield to improve their negotiating position.

Therefore, at times in secret and at times very much under the full glare of international perusal, the war went on. Far beneath the surface, however, as far as Pretoria was concerned at least, was the growing interdependency of South Africa and UNITA. While there may have been considerable official secrecy surrounding this policy, in practical terms it had become more or less common knowledge.

As the year progressed and as international diplomacy limped from one blind alley to another, press speculation began to dwell more frequently on the extent of combined operations underway between the SADF and UNITA. The Angolan news agency Angop claimed on 12 August 1983 that eight SAAF aircraft – four Canberras and four Impala ground-strike fighters – had repeatedly bombed and destroyed the small but strategically important rail and communication centre of Cangamba in the southeast Moxico Province. Although little more than a scattering of thatch and iron-roofed buildings some 500 kilometres north of the South West African border, Cangamba included a functional airstrip that was seen by both UNITA and the MPLA as being of vital strategic importance, and from where the Angolans were tactically able to launch air assaults against Savimbi's main force concentrations in the southeast. At the time, the MPLA was defending the settlement against a determined and bitter effort by UNITA to gain control of it.

The SADF dismissed the Angolan claim as fanciful but the Angolans persisted, speculating further that SADF troops still garrisoning Xangongo and Ongiva had been massively reinforced, and repeatedly claiming that South African troops were active in Moxico Province in eastern–central Angola in direct support of UNITA. And while all of this had a clear histrionic ring to it, there was no doubt that something was afoot in the region – a region that South Africa obviously had no direct strategic interest in – and no less clear that somehow or other South African was involved.

UNITA certainly had by then grown into a significant force in east and southern–central Angola. This gave it practical control about 25 per cent of the whole country, almost the entire southeast quadrant, with an additional operational presence on a more or

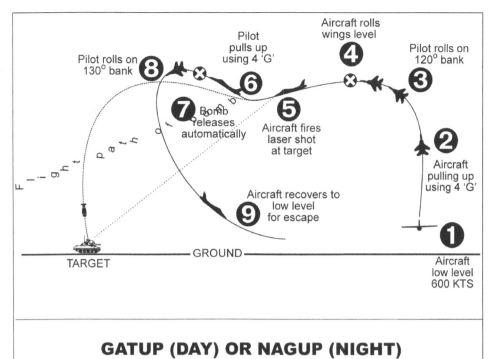

Pilot rolls on
130° bank

Pilot
pulls up
using 4 'G'

Aircraft rolls
wings level

Pilot rolls on
120° bank

Bomb
releases
automatically

Aircraft fires
laser shot
at target

Aircraft
pulling up
using 4 'G'

Aircraft recovers to
low level
for escape

GROUND

TARGET

Aircraft
low level
600 KTS

GATUP (DAY) OR NAGUP (NIGHT)

The mercurial Bossie Huyser, commander
of Western Air Command.

less continuous basis in another 50 per cent. This fact, even at the time, was tacitly acknowledged by the central government in Luanda and broadly acknowledged elsewhere. By then, UNITA claimed to have some 35,000 trained and semi-trained fighters in the field. It was well supported by such African states as Zaire and Zambia and, of course, South Africa, with more covert but nonetheless influential support emanating from the United States.

Direct South Africa military support for UNITA – military advisers in the wonderfully opaque political language of the time – offered a clear and tangible strategic benefit for South Africa. In the first instance, UNITA's military adventures diverted and preoccupied FAPLA and, to an increasing degree, SWAPO too, relieving the SADF of the need to directly defend the Eastern Front, or the long Caprivi–Kavango border region. In certain quarters it was speculated that perhaps South Africa now needed UNITA more than UNITA needed her.

This fact was not, of course, lost on Savimbi, who certainly did capitalize on it frequently by petitioning Pretoria for material and military assistance. Such requests would usually be followed by the SAAF providing VIP air transport for Savimbi to visit either Pretoria or Cape Town, which would then be further followed by a top-secret signal to the SADF detailing the practical assistance that was to be provided.

In the matter of the battle for Cangamba there have been many conflicting reports on the extent to which South Africa was involved. According to UNITA's own version, after six months of starving out the 3,000 MPLA defenders, Savimbi began the battle on 3 August 1983 by shelling the town with some of the Soviet-made 76mm artillery pieces that had been captured three years earlier. He then sent in several battalion-strength detachments of semi-conventional troops as well as irregulars and 'commandos'. Over eight days of heavy fighting UNITA suffered serious losses from mines and strafing from MiGs and Mi-8 attack helicopters operating from Luena and against which UNITA could offer little

in the way of practical defence. But by mid-August, the defences of Cangamba had been so comprehensively compromised that more than 100 surviving Cubans were airlifted out by helicopter. Cangamba was finally taken on 14 August at a heavy cost in UNITA and MPLA/Cuban lives.

Although no mention of the fact is made in the preceding account, according to Brigadier-General Dick Lord, Savimbi did indeed request active South African assistance in the battle, claiming that, although the area around the town had been cleared, the MPLA HQ itself remained occupied and functioning and that without immediate help the likelihood was that UNITA would soon need to withdraw. Bearing mind that the scene of this battle lay significantly outside of SWAPO's and South Africa's sphere of activity, the request was received with caution. Direct South African involvement could hardly have been construed as anything other than an overt intervention in the Angolan civil war. A meeting of high-level South African sectorial commanders was quickly convened and the matter subjected to much discussion.

> Huyser [*Brigadier 'Bossie' Huyser,* commander of Western Air Command] attended this meeting and listened to all the arguments for and against. When negotiations reached stalemate Huyser jumped into the whirlpool with both feet and said, "Give authority to the SAAF for one airstrike and UNITA will take Cangamba!" Silence greeted his career-jeopardizing announcement but, after consideration, the authority was given.[17]

With this, the reputation of the SAAF was on the line as, no doubt, was the personal reputation and future career prospects of Brigadier Bossie Huyser himself. However, with minute planning and the hope of a fair wind behind it, Operation *Karton* went into effect early in the morning of 14 August, utilizing Buccaneers and Canberras from 3, 12 and 24 squadrons. The attack succeeded in what has since come to be regarded as one of the most effective and well-executed operations of its kind undertaken at any time during the war. Within a few hours, the final walk-in took place and Cangamba was in UNITA hands. The negative result – for there always seemed to be one of these, often the same one – was an immediate and significant escalation in the amount and sophistication of Soviet replacement weaponry shipped to Angola and channelled to the front, as well as the arrival in the country of an additional investment of several thousand Cuban troops.

In the short term, however, the UNITA position in the southeast had been buttressed and the SADF could return its attention to dealing with a new arc of SWAPO/FAPLA brigade positions established north of the Shallow Area since the completion of Operation *Protea*, and located variously at Cahama, Cuvelai, Caindo in the north of the Cunene Province and Mulondo in the adjacent Huila Province. Intelligence soon began to seep south that PLAN intended to launch its heaviest infiltration thus far into South West Africa as soon as the 1983/84 wet season commenced. To counter this, the SADF began planning for Operation *Askari*, a follow-up to Operation *Protea* and perhaps one of the most important major combined external operations of the war.

Operation *Askari* was earmarked for launch in mid-November 1983, unusual timing, bearing in mind that it would correspond more or less with the onset of the wet season and all the difficulties associated with mounting a mechanized operation in southern Angola in the teeth of the annual rains.

It is worth noting in this regard that the cycle of war in the region tended to correspond more or less with seasonal variations of rainfall and drought. The tropical/subtropical weather system of southern Africa follows a pattern of summer rainfall – often in a short and a long phase – occurring annually between late November and February/March and a dry winter season that peaks between the months of June and September. During the wet season, heat and humidity levels tend to be high while veld conditions are lush with rich ground cover and heavy tree foliage, and with a tendency also for there to be large expanses of shallow standing water in alkaline pans known locally as shonas.[18]

Since the earliest days of European activity in the region, it has always been understood that the dry winter season is the time for warfare and ambulation. Wheeled transport is feasible on untreated road surfaces only at this time, while cool conditions and a paucity of disease-carrying parasites such as mosquitoes and tsetse flies render human and animal movement much more practical. During the wet summer months, however, the opposite has always been true: bushveld conditions become impossible for the movement of livestock and wagons, and in later years motor vehicles, while high levels of humidity and rain tend to see correspondingly high levels of lethargy, discomfort and disease, particularly among non-natives.

It therefore made perfect sense for SWAPO units to disperse into the countryside and begin the long overland journey south from its forward bases as the rains set in. For them the principal hazard was malaria, but certainly not limits on vehicle transport, since a bulk of the journey would be undertaken on foot and, besides which, any limitations on SADF capacity to mobilize would always be an advantage. Perhaps a greater advantage than this was the large expanses of standing water scattered across the bushveld, without which long-distance deployment over an otherwise parched and arid landscape would have been suicidal. Flooded shonas also offered the opportunity for small groups of guerrillas moving through any given area the opportunity to obscure their tracks by hopping from one flooded pan to another, with the additional advantage of regular downpours washing away what tracks they did leave. Moreover, thick savannah woodland of the type common throughout southern Angola would usually be bare of foliage in the dry season, but heavily canopied during the rains which helped in the matter of concealment both from ground patrols and from the air.

Conversely, for the SADF, large mechanized columns became an utter liability in the rough and undeveloped conditions of southern Angola during the wet season, which meant that the style of operations during this period was likely to be limited to containment, tracking and follow-up foot patrols in the border area.

At the onset of the dry season, however, most SWAPO units would be recalled from the field for what was termed 'rehearsals' which saw them concentrated in bases, perfect circumstances for the launch of large-scale offensive operations to deal with them in numbers.

The planning for Operation *Askari* also went ahead against these and other difficulties, among them international pressure, as well as a great deal of concern in Pretoria regarding another bout of re-armament in Angola in the aftermath of the most recent destruction wrought in Cangamba. The arrival in Luanda had been observed of at least ten Russian cargo ships packed to the gunwales with everything from T-62 battle tanks to helicopters and high-altitude anti-aircraft missiles. In addition, Cuba shipped over 5,000 fresh troops, bringing the total based in Angola to a South African estimate, probably conservative, of 25,000.

At more or less the same time, United Nations Secretary-General Perez de Cuellar undertook a lightning familiarization tour of the affected countries, spending two days in Pretoria before flying north to Luanda where he was personally received by Angolan President José Eduardo dos Santos, and later introduced to Sam Nujoma, whom he referred to on the steps of the presidential palace as "the representative of the Namibian people". This, of course, all combined to increase the sense in Pretoria that the entire negotiated process was stacked against South Africa, which was probably not the case in practical terms but in moral terms it certainly was.

Likewise, the threat of a more direct Soviet intervention on the side of Angola appeared to be growing as the scale and severity of South African operations grew. Demands for the removal of the semi-permanent garrison of South African troops in Xangongo and Ongiva were also frequently being heard, not least from the Americans who, as much as they did not want to commit troops to the theatre themselves, also did not want the Soviets to have

Mechanized SADF troops taking a breather.
Photo courtesy Cameron Blake.

An Alouette III up close and personal with SADF ground troops.
Photo courtesy Cameron Blake.

any excuse to do so. It was impossible, of course, to hide the fact that the South Africans were planning *something*. The pace of air-reconnaissance flights over any given area in Angola could always be regarded as fair warning of that, and as South African aircraft began to appear with greater frequency in the skies over southern Angola in preparation for Operation *Askari*, Moscow issued a quiet warning to Pretoria that an expansion of the war, such as might be about to take place, would carry with it a significant risks for South Africa.

The warning came in the form of a written dispatch handed to South African diplomats – the precise venue for this is not known but it was probably in Washington or at the United Nations – by their Soviet counterparts, to be passed on to the government in Pretoria. While it was stressed in the dispatch that the contents of the message should not be regarded as a threat, it was nonetheless pointed out that the continued occupation of Angolan territory by South Africa and ongoing support for UNITA were unacceptable to Moscow. Moreover, it was stated that the desired withdrawal of Cuban troop from Angola as a precondition for the extraction of South African troops from South West Africa would not take place. The USSR, it was pointed out, was tied to Angola by an agreement of friendship and cooperation and could be expected to provide what support was required by Angola for the protection of its sovereignty and territorial integrity.

Needless to say, Pretoria rebuffed this threat, which it clearly was, while the final planning and preparation for Operation *Askari* went ahead. The South Africans were nonetheless rattled by the exchange. The offensive aspects of the plan were as a consequence modified, with the main objective once again being to disrupt and destroy SWAPO's logistics, deployment and supply capability, but this time the emphasis was placed on a strategy of isolating military strongpoints and applying threat and attrition in the hope that enemy forces would suffer a collapse of morale and desert without the necessity of a full confrontation. The operational plan was finally approved in four phases:

Phase 1: Deep penetration Special Force reconnaissance followed by SAAF air assault on the Typhoon/Volcano[19] base located near Lubango, taking place between 1 November and 30 December 1983;

Phase 2: Offensive reconnaissance operations and the isolation of Cahama, Mulondo and Cuvelai, extending from 16 November 1983 to mid-January 1984. The aim of this was to cut off enemy communication and logistic lines in what was known as the Deep Area, or all areas of Angola which were of operational interest to South Africa but not within the defined Shallow Area. This, it was hoped, would demoralize and terrorize SWAPO defenders to the extent that they would abandon their positions and withdraw northward;

Phase 3: Commencing at the beginning of February 1984, to establish a dominated area from west of the Cunene River, through Quiteve, Mupa, Vinticette and eastward through Ionde;

Phase 4: The final curtailment of hostile incursions into South West Africa, internally if required.

The three principal targets of Operation *Askari* were located in a wide arc within what was classified by FAPLA as its 5th Military Region. Cahama, one of the main proposed targets, lay 150 kilometres northwest of Xangongo on what at the time was a good road, while Mulondo, another key target, was located a little farther than this, perhaps 200 kilometres from Xangongo, but also on an accessible arterial route. Cuvelai lay farther north still but was considerably more remote on the eastern perimeter of the derelict *Parque Nacional da Mupa*.

A heavy Special Force reconnaissance insertion, one of the largest so far in the war, was done at a number of points behind enemy lines in order to gather the necessary tactical intelligence on enemy strengths and dispositions upon which detailed planning could be made. What was reported back in general terms was that FAPLA was at brigade strength at Cahama, Mulondo and Cuvelai – with a brigade in this context being somewhere between 600 and 1,000 men. In addition, each town was well defended by an extensive network of bunkers as well as a great deal of razor wire, minefields and artillery. Of particular concern to the flying crews were the well-integrated anti-aircraft defences that included a brace of SA-8s and SA-9 missile systems as well as 14.5mm and 23mm guns. However, the entire configuration,

The venerable grand dame of the SAAF: a Dakota coming in to land.

A stick of Mk 82 250kg bombs doing their job.

in keeping perhaps with the Soviet doctrine that inspired it, was clearly defensive in intent, suggesting that there was only a very limited potential for any direct offensive action on the ground.

What was also ascertained – although separate reports differ on this fact – and notwithstanding a handful of Cuban and Soviet advisers in situ, was that no meaningful foreign element to PLAN/FAPLA forces was in place. A Cuban regiment was based at Jamba, however, and a second at Matala, both in the Huíla Province north of the main focus of SADF attention.

Offensive action against Cahama began in mid-November with an initial deployment of Special Force reconnaissance teams to cut logistics and communication lines and to generally attempt the isolation of Cahama while the SAAF carried out strikes against identified targets within the defensive perimeter. The strategy was to rattle and exhaust defending forces prior to the additional psychological stress of realizing, with the arrival of the main mechanized force, that a major South African attack was imminent.

This preliminary softening-up had a limited effect, as Brigadier-General Dick Lord commented in his history of the SAAF in the Border War, *From Fledgling to Eagle*, because a garrison such as that entrenched in Cahama, fortified by the sense that it had beaten the *Boere* back on previous encounters, was hardly likely to be overawed by the offensive efforts of a handful of Recces and the attentions of the SAAF against its well-constructed trench and bunker system. It was not until the forward advance of Task Force X-Ray, comprising mainly 61 Mechanized Battalion and attached artillery, and with a SAAF MAOT attached, appeared in mid-December that the real pressure began to be applied. (*See* appendix for a first-hand account of a SAAF officer serving as MAOT for 61 Mechanized Battalion during Operation *Askari*.)

In this regard, it is worth noting that Cahama had been heavily and consistently bombed during earlier operations – particularly during Operation *Protea* – although it had never been targeted with a view to being taken or occupied, which had always tended to be interpreted by the enemy as a tactical loss, with much subsequent propaganda mileage being made out of this fact by the defenders who consistently claimed that they had driven off the *Boere*.

Another point worth mentioning in regard to the assault

on Cahama is the fact that it was known prior to the launch of *Askari* that among the anti-aircraft armaments deployed around the target was the vehicle-mounted and radar-supported Soviet SA-8 missile system, a highly mobile, low-altitude, short-range, tactical surface-to-air missile system that until then had not been deployed outside of the USSR. The capture of one of these was the objective of a high-priority side operation codenamed *Fox*. This operation involved coordinated ground and air bombardments undertaken in such a way as to force the southward movement of the mobile batteries in order that an SA-8 could be isolated by ground forces and snatched. The operation failed, although an older SA-9 system was captured in Cuvelai which, even though not precisely what was hoped for, was nonetheless an important acquisition and of significant intelligence interest.

In the meanwhile, prior to the advance of Task Force X-Ray, comprising mainly 61 Mechanized Battalion and attached artillery, on the outskirts of Cahama, it successfully overran the small defended town of Quiteve against almost no resistance. This prompted an unsuccessful probe north by a detached company of Task Force X-Ray to begin the process of isolating Mulondo. This caused some grumbling from SAAF command as it required the unscheduled diversion of air resources to support the advance which reduced the cover available elsewhere. Brigadier-General Dick Lord:

> This diversion of the original Askari plan had repercussions on the air plan. Support had to be flown for ground forces in that area, thus utilizing aircraft hours and weapons set aside for the Cahama and Cuvelai battles. It had a further tactical disadvantage in that the element of surprise we had hoped to gain from our attack on Cahama was lost. After our Mulondo strikes the entire air defence system of southern Angola was placed on the highest state of alert.[20]

Cahama, meanwhile, was now subjected to an unrelenting artillery bombardment during the day and night/day aerial attacks delivered by Impala and Canberra formations that lasted throughout the second half of December. In the midst of these

A pair of Mirage F1s in mountainous terrain.

ACM debrief. From left: Jeronkie Venter, Wayne Smal, Alan Brand and Rudi Mes.

raids a flight of Buccaneers was diverted briefly to attack SWAPO/FAPLA forward training and logistics bases near the town of Lubango on the main road north of Cahama.

The combined effect of weeks of intense attrition applied to Cahama certainly did affect morale among the defenders, as had been hoped, with radio intercepts confirming this fact, and had the operation been allowed to continue it would certainly have succeeded. However, all SADF operations around Cahama were abruptly ordered to cease by 31 December, largely as a consequence of international pressure being brought to bear against the South African government to withdraw its forces from Angola. This had the melancholy effect of allowing the FAPLA 2nd Brigade in Cahama to observe one morning, to their unutterable relief, the mighty SADF 61 Mechanized Battalion breaking the siege and leaving the area, with the predictable result that yet another defeat of the *Boere* was hailed by FAPLA. Similarly, the combined offensive plan against Mulondo was discontinued.

In the midst of the Cahama siege, however air assets were once again diverted when a Sector 20 SADF deception force was attacked and five members killed during an unscheduled diversionary strike at a position close to the town of Caiundo, more than 200 kilometres east of the main combat zone. The SAAF had not been informed of this aspect to the operation and therefore had not factored in any contingency for dealing with this sort of emergency. Air activity was now spread even more thinly, with attack aircraft being diverted to Caiundo from both Cahama and Mulondo in the midst of the campaign to suppress both. Caiundo remained a focus of air activity for the remainder of the life of Operation *Askari*, itself ultimately not being captured and contributing to the similar marginal failures at Cahama and Mulondo.

At 14h05 on 27 December 1983, the aerial bombardment of the final key target, Cuvelai, north of Xangongo, began. This followed a week or more of photo-reconnaissance flights which had warned the defenders of the town well in advance that something big was imminent. The aerial attacks continued for the next few days, after which Task Force Delta-Fox, a battle group comprising mainly territorial Citizen Force soldiers, was sent in to engage a SWAPO HQ and logistics base located five kilometres northeast

of the town. To its horror, the group came under attack from the FAPLA 11th Brigade, reinforced by two Cuban battalions, and utilizing T-54/T-55 tanks for the first time in their correct mobile role. Task Force X-Ray was immediately reassigned to assist and in a mere 16 hours was extracted from its activity around Cahama and redeployed overland to the outskirts of Cuvelai. This epic forced march is described in part by Captain Charlie Wroth in the appendix. There a combined ground and air assault commenced on 3 January 1984.

Supporting air operations began with a determined and coordinated series of strikes aimed at all known AAA and artillery sites. The first wave comprised ten Impala jets followed by four Canberras. The combined load of bombs delivered on the target was 60 120kg bombs, 18 350kg bombs, two 460kg bombs and 600 deadly anti-personnel alpha bombs, followed by a second wave of Impalas dropping 32 250kg bombs. Each pilot was equipped with an up-to-date aerial photograph of his intended target and a high degree of accuracy was achieved.

This was confirmed on completion of the air attack by an intercepted radio call from the Angolan commander pleading for help from his HQ in Lubango, claiming that 75 per cent of his artillery had been taken out by the SAAF. If this was even partially so then this certainly would have ranked highly among SAAF actions during the war. Dick Lord, remarking on this fact, commented that: "This airstrike, together with the Cangamba attack, ranks arguably as the two most successful airstrikes flown by the SAAF throughout the history of the war."[21]

During the air operation an Impala piloted by Captain Joe van den Berg was clipped in the tail by an SA-9 missile, completely destroying the right side tail-plane and elevator. A combination of skilled piloting and controlled elevation loss allowed the aircraft to land safely at the recently resurfaced airstrip at Ongiva.

The SAAF, meanwhile, continued to fly in support of ground troops moving in on Cuvelai, with Alouette pilot Captain Carl Alberts winning the Honoris Crux for marking gun positions under heavy fire, evading, so the story is told, four simultaneously fired RPG rockets. After labouring through the extensive minefields surrounding the town, and losing a Ratel to a T-55 hit that resulted in the death of ten men, ground forces entered Cuvelai to find that both SWAPO and FAPLA had fled, later running into 32 Battalion stop groups positioned south of Tetchamutete where a handful were killed and many more captured. Eleven enemy tanks were taken out during the battle, with an estimated 324 Angolan and Cuban lives lost.

It need hardly be said that Operation *Askari* stirred up a ferment of hyperbolic but hardly exaggerated pleas on the part of the Angolans and gales of outrage from the international community. All of this the South Africans deflected with as much stone-faced denial as was possible, but with, nonetheless, a finger on the pulse of the wider international reaction to gauge the point at which the operation would need to be brought to a close.

Mopping up was still underway in Cuvelai when news reached Pretoria of a dispatch between SWAPO leader Sam Nujoma and UN Secretary-General Perez de Cuellar, pleading for the latter to arrange a direct ceasefire between the SADF and his own forces in order to "contribute meaningfully to an early ceasefire agreement".

This was obviously done under pressure from the reeling Angolans and as such was something of a red herring. There had been throughout the liberation period in recent African history many similar incidences where pleas such as this were simply used as an opportunity for rearming, regrouping and the reoccupation of territory defined as demilitarized by any ceasefire agreement. It was simply a fact of the times.

Phase 3 of Operation *Askari*, the establishment of a dominated area between the Cunene and Cubango rivers and as far north Tetchamutete, had been achieved, although the area west of the Cunene remained broadly hostile. The success of Phase 4 – the halting of the annual SWAPO incursion – is subjective, and can be measured only in terms of insurgent and SADF deaths in the area of border operations in the weeks and months that followed. An incursion in 1984 did take place, so SWAPO activity was certainly not halted, although it was undoubtedly a less ambitious penetration than had originally been planned.

By 15 January, the last of the raiding forces had crossed back into South West Africa where the planners and commanders of the operation could step back and ponder what really had been very mixed results. On the whole, however, *Askari* was deemed a success, in particular when measured using the yardstick of enemy losses and the accumulation or destruction of astronomical quantities of war booty. (It was frequently remarked, obviously, but not wholly fallaciously, that, under a general and increasing arms embargo, the Soviets remained the largest supplier of arms to South Africa. Indeed, South Africa did make practical use of many articles of captured hardware in the form of vehicles, artillery and some aircraft.) Also, of course, another significant blow had been delivered to the logistical and deployment capability of SWAPO which, although diminishing the organization's short-term effectiveness on the battlefield, it did nothing to significantly alter the overall trajectory of either the situation or the pace and intensity of the war.

In fact, the South Africans had much to reflect upon as 1984 dawned that must at the time have seemed quite depressing. South African troops in the battle for Cuvelai had for the first time encountered tanks used in their correct mobile capacity and, although still not deployed with quite the level of skill necessary to defeat a force on a par with the SADF, it still marked a turning point on the battlefield that would no doubt develop further. It was also evident that Angolan, Cuban and Soviet commitment to the defence of Angolan territory had been markedly more aggressive during this operation than at any previous time which again could be expected to increase as the situation unfolded. Lastly, there remained a residual unease occasioned by the Soviet threat of robust intervention should the South African presence in Angola ever become more overtly threatening than it had been hitherto, unease that remained strong with the ongoing South African occupation of Xangongo and Ongiva.

CHAPTER NINE:
A DEEPER INVOLVEMENT IN THE ANGOLAN CIVIL WAR

Since Operation *Savannah* of 1975 there had in effect been two wars underway in Angola – the civil war between UNITA and the MPLA, in which South Africa and SWAPO were involved, and the border insurgency between South Africa and SWAPO in which UNITA and the MPLA were involved. The complexity of this battlefield was reflected by the no less convoluted twists and turns of the parallel political roadmap. Consider, for example, the contradictory relationship the Reagan administration in Washington sustained with the MPLA. The United States was Angola's most important foreign trading partner, thanks in large part to oil exploitation and export, mainly in the hands of Chevron, making Angola the United States' fourth-largest trading partner on the continent. At the same time as Washington was resolutely refusing recognition to the MPLA and funding UNITA as a counter-balance, she was also pouring funds into the central treasury that bankrolled Angolan arms purchases which in turn helped arm the huge Cuban military presence which Washington steadfastly held must be withdrawn.

The internal situation in South Africa was also reaching a point of critical load. The militarization of the country, the internationalization of the anti-apartheid movement and South Africa's growing international isolation, coupled with periodic eruptions of township violence and protest – such as that occasioned by the shooting dead of 19 black protesters on 21 March 1984 as the 25th anniversary of the Sharpeville Massacre was commemorated – all tended to add to the sense of inevitability

The 'office' of an Alouette gunship.

FAPA (Angolan Air Force) Mi-8 helicopters at Cuvelai, southern Angola, 1984.

of change in the country and a deep feeling of disquiet as to what form that change would take.

And somewhat predictably the simplicity of the original terms of the UN-proposed ceasefire in the midst of Operation *Askari* were now mired in a slew of amendments, demands, counter-demands, acceptances, refusals and contradictory political statements, all of which did nothing to clear the opacity of the situation, offering South Africa no surety whatsoever that the ground upon which she was reluctantly forced to tread had any real diplomatic substance.

However, on 13 February 1984, high-level South African, Angolan and United States delegations met in Lusaka for two days of intensive talks which resulted in the drafting of a document known as the Mulungushi Minute. This document, little more than a nine-point memorandum, established a Joint Monitoring Commission to observe the disengagement process of each belligerent and to detect, investigate and report any infringements or violations thereof. The plan defined an Area in Question that was to be cleared of both South African and SWAPO military presence. It was to be bounded in the south by the South West African/Namibian border and in the north by an imaginary line that ran west to east from the Marienflüss near the Cunene River mouth to Iona, Mulondo, a point ten kilometres north of Cassinga, the Cubango River and then southward following the river back to the South West African/Namibian border. In broad terms, no SADF troops would be permitted north of the Joint Monitoring Commission HQ which was in fact mobile. The Area in Question would be comprehensively swept to ensure the removal of both SWAPO and SADF/SWAFT elements, after which it would be occupied by FAPLA.

Neither the Angolans nor SWAPO in the event put any meaningful effort into the implementation of the plan. The MPLA was still highly dependent on both Cuban and SWAPO military support to contain the expansion of UNITA and, moreover, for reasons of a future security buffer along its southern boundary, it was extremely cool to any possibility of a future for South West Africa/Namibia that did not include a SWAPO government. SWAPO, of course, had absolutely no intention of abandoning or even curtailing its infiltration into South West Africa, not, it

must be said with any expectation of a military victory, but simply to avoid abandoning its claim to be *primus inter pares* in the eyes of the UN and the wider global community. Needless to say, armed clashes continued both in the border area and throughout the Area in Question which led South Africa – itself highly sceptical of progress and possibly facing the uncomfortable 'next step' of negotiations with SWAPO – also to drag her feet. The implementation of United Nations Resolution 435, no matter what other creative diplomacy might periodically surface and subside, would not take place until a Cuban withdrawal from Angola, which would not take place until a South African withdrawal from South West Africa. And there the matter remained.

By the end of the year, just one flotsam of truth was visible above this ocean of obfuscation when Angolan President José Eduardo dos Santos published a remark to the effect that, notwithstanding whatever else might take place, some Cuban troops would need to remain in Angola, even after Namibian independence. He stated: "Angola cannot make concessions which amount to suicide for its national integrity and socio-political development." This gave final truth to the fact that Cuban intervention, where once it had been aimed at protecting Angola from the predations of South Africa, was now even more vital to keep in check the ambitions of Jonas Savimbi and UNITA, without which the MPLA government would have little real chance of survival.

UNITA had also become the principal South African preoccupation of the war, with most SAAF activity during 1984 and 1985 focused on providing logistical assistance in one form or another to Savimbi's forces in recognition of the vital role the movement was playing in securing the key southeast quarter of Angola closest to South West Africa. An example of the kind of work that the SAAF was now undertaking on behalf of UNITA was Operation *Magneto*, staged between 23 August and 10 September, to assist UNITA in the large-scale transport of troops to airfields at Gago Couthino and Cazombo in an attempt to thwart a major Angolan effort to retake the Cazombo Enclave which at that time lay under UNITA control. SAAF MAOTs were positioned at each airfield to control flying operations, all of which were undertaken by Pumas or elements of the C-130/C-160 fleet, flying collectively 220 hours on delivery flights and 30 hours of helicopter support. All flights were undertaken at night because of the risk of MiG interception.

Then, in a replay of the parody of the 'Grand Old Duke of York', Operation *Wallpaper*, staged between 11 September and 8 October, extracted large numbers of UNITA personnel from Cazombo once the situation there had become untenable and FAPLA successfully occupied the enclave, with the SAAF returning the UNITA troops to the Mavinga area in order to counter a southeasterly thrust of the Angolan advance toward Savimbi's powerbase and centre of operations at Jamba.[22]

In both operations SAAF crews found themselves dealing with very primitive conditions, with the SAAF MAOT using a portable VHF radio for air-traffic control on extremely basic runway conditions and with runway lights being provided by burning tin cans filled with sand and primed with kerosene. Aircraft engines were kept running throughout loading and unloading in order to minimize the risk of failures and the disastrous potential of aircraft standing on unprotected runways in broad daylight as sitting ducks for patrolling MiGs.

These flights were sustained and successful despite extreme operational pressure. Night flying ensured invisibility while a narrow radar gap that existed in regionally located systems allowed the South African aircraft, for the most part, to slip in and out of the region undetected by enemy or friendly air-space surveillance.[23]

Parallel to Operation *Wallpaper*, Operation *Weldmesh* was authorized as it became clear that the Angolan advance against Mavinga/Jamba – codename *Second Congress* by the Angolans – heavily supported by a fleet of Angolan MiGs, Soviet-made Mi-25 helicopter gunships/troop transports and Mi-17 transport helicopters, was threatening to overrun Mavinga. This would have led to a rapid collapse of UNITA's dominance in the vital Cuando Cubango Province, adjacent to the Caprivi Strip and South Africa's effective Eastern Front.

Weldmesh involved a major aerial bombardment by Canberra, Buccaneer, Mirage and Impala fighter-bombers which devastated the FAPLA brigades, forcing them back toward Cuito Cuanavale. These were in addition to heavy and accurate artillery bombardment from an SADF ground force deployed to counter the weight of armour used by Angolan government forces. A number of SADF members were on attachment to UNITA as advisers, while Recce and 32 Battalion teams were active in reconnaissance and ambush roles.

This combined SADF intervention broke the back of the Angolan advance, allowing UNITA to immediately launch into harassing attacks on the retreating forces. The interception of Angolan radio communications indicated that FAPLA had requested helicopter assistance for the removal of casualties back to their medical centres, flights that were later ascertained to have been used instead to evacuate Soviet military personnel. This presented the SAAF with something of an opportunity. The Soviets were the brains behind much of the planning and execution of *Second Congress* and their removal, or at least the removal of as many as possible, would seriously impact the conduct of the operation.

It was established that the Angolan helicopters were operating out of Menongue and for the most part well below SAAF radar cover. A ground-reconnaissance team from 32 Battalion was inserted into the area to monitor the movement of helicopter traffic in and out of the base. While Mirage F1CZ fighters were deployed to AFB Rundu to provide close air support to the reconnaissance team should it be needed, it was decided to use Impalas to intercept the Angolan helicopters once information had been received that they were airborne in the operational zone.

Several missions were aborted either before or after take-off when it was established that the timing of the flight was not optimum. The first successful strike took place late in the afternoon of 27 September when two Mi-25 attack helicopters were observed taking off and heading toward the war zone. Both were shot down by SAAF Impalas.

Two days later the 32 Battalion ground team observed the departure of a second helicopter formation comprising two Mi-8/-17 transport helicopters, escorted by two Mi-24 gunships. Once again the Impalas were scrambled and all four helicopters were brought down. Two MiG-23 fighters were observed flying at about 200 feet above the debris of the stricken helicopters but no hostile action was attempted. No further helicopter resupply, rescue and evacuation were attempted by the Angolans.

CHAPTER TEN:
CUITO CUANAVALE: THE LAST MILITARY CHAPTER

Throughout the 1980s UNITA continued to extend and consolidate its control over an ever-widening swath of territory, reaching northward along the eastern flank of Angola toward the border with Zaire, eventually leading to speculation that Savimbi might be planning to move his main headquarters from Jamba in the southeast to an unspecified location closer to the Zairean border. It was here, in fact, that the United States had begun refurbishing a long-established airbase located outside the southern Zairean town of Kamina as an alternative supply route to the now dangerously attenuated Mavinga line of aerial communication used by UNITA to receive South African support.[24]

This in turn led to a great deal of nervous discussion in Pretoria that UNITA might now be sufficiently fledged to abandon its links with South Africa altogether which, of course, no matter how buoyant Savimbi might have been about his military prospects, was extremely unlikely. Since the ignominious collapse of Operation

The Cuito bridge.

Much loathed by FAPLA and PLAN, the Seeker RPV in flight.

Angolan Mi-24s.

The centre-line tank can be jettisoned to transform the Mirage F1CZ into a sleek fighter.

Second Congress, another bout of Angolan rearming and tactical re-evaluation had seen a massive increase in FAPLA's offensive capacity. It the words of war historian Willem Steenkamp:

> Fresh supplies of weapons and equipment were flowing into Angola on a daily basis: tanks, guns, armoured fighting vehicles, radars, fighters and fighter-bombers, helicopter gunships, air-defence rockets – some of the items so modern that Western evaluation experts had never laid hands on them. The Soviet Union was like a martial cornucopia, showering Angola with a king's ransom in military hardware (… the equivalent of R2 billions' worth between mid-1986 and mid-1987).

A handful of foreign correspondents were also allowed to glimpse preparations underway, each describing scenes of Soviet aerial transports shuttling in to various air facilities in Angola and disgorging an unending weight of military equipment. Notwithstanding Savimbi's US-supplied Stinger missiles and much rhetorical support from his regional allies, only South Africa had the capacity and inclination to provide the sort of fighting assets to counter the sheer weight of armaments that would face UNITA in the event of another major FAPLA offensive.

In fact, it became quite clear as 1987 progressed that preparations for a second major push against the UNITA strongholds of Mavinga and Jamba were indeed underway. Much of the incoming equipment and matériel arriving in the country was being channelled down and stockpiled at Menongue, before being moved on to Cuito Cuanavale along with significant troop concentrations. In addition, the planning and command

capabilities of FAPLA had been greatly enhanced by a large number of – estimates suggest over 1,000 – Soviet advisers, including the high-ranking appointee General Konstantin Shaganovitch.

Shaganovitch appears to have arrived on the scene in an effort to divert the possibility of another grandiose Angolan defeat. To date, the Soviets had invested an astronomical amount of money in the outcome of the Angolan civil war, far more than could simply be written off, and despite his general policy of rapprochement with the West, Gorbachev agreed to throw good money after bad and underwrite another massive Angolan military operation to dislodge and finally destroy UNITA. However, in order to limit as much as possible the debilitating incompetence of the Angolans, Shaganovitch was appointed supreme commander of all MPLA forces, although reports vary on the extent to which he had any direct command over the large Cuban force in the country.

In August 1987, FAPLA commenced *Operação Saludando Octubre*, or Operation *Greeting October*, with the launch of four (some sources claim five) brigades, including the armoured 47th Brigade, from Cuito Cuanavale, moving south directly toward Mavinga. Savimbi lodged an immediate plea for South African assistance which was not particularly welcome at a highly sensitive political juncture. Cabinet approval was eventually given, however, but only once the Angolan 47th Brigade had crossed the Lomba River, a point no more than 20 kilometres north of Mavinga from where it clearly posed a threat to both Mavinga and Jamba.

With customary political indifference to practical military capacity, the SADF was blithely instructed to halt the FAPLA offensive and buttress UNITA's power base with the proviso that no manpower or equipment must be lost and that South African involvement must be both secret and plausibly deniable. The reply was made that this was manifestly impossible; casualties would be sustained and, moreover, if there was to be any hope of success, G5 howitzers and tanks would be required.

This was a moment of profound decision for South Africa. All things considered – bearing in mind not only the ongoing political exchanges surrounding the implementation of Resolution 435, an expanding internal protest movement and the tightening arms embargo that affected the precious SAAF fighter fleet more than anything – this was a lot to ask. The last time the SADF, then the UDF, had deployed tanks in battle was during the drive north through Italy in the closing phases of the Second World War.

UNITA, however, was clearly crumbling against the determined FAPLA advance and the stakes were high. Authority was given for 32 Battalion with enhanced armour and artillery support – although without G5s or tanks – to be deployed to Mavinga in an operation codenamed *Modular*.

In the meanwhile, an extraordinarily daring Special Force reconnaissance operation, Operation *Coolidge*, was undertaken to destroy the vital road bridge over the Cuito River, immediately east of Cuito Cuanavale, which was vital for the movement south of the heavy FAPLA armoured brigades and other motorized units and, perhaps interestingly and more devastatingly still, logistical resupply and support once the main armoured brigades had already crossed the river heading south.

On the night of 25/26 August a combat swimming team comprising 12 operators equipped with collapsible Klepper canoes was dropped by SAAF Pumas 70 kilometres upriver of Cuito Cuanavale from where, by a combination of swimming and paddling, they made their way downriver to the site of the Cuito River Bridge . The group was compromised as soon as they approached the target but, nonetheless, laid their charges under hostile fire before retreating farther downriver while being pursued from the bank and fired at. Moreover, as if all this was not enough, a crocodile attack resulted in a dreadful life-and-death struggle for one member who survived by displaying almost unimaginable cool in what must have been terrifying circumstances, stabbing the creature with his fighting knife until he was released.

Thereafter survival became a matter of keeping ahead of the enemy in a desperate chase through flat and uniform savannah bushveld with the enemy close on their heels. Four SAAF Pumas aborted the first pick-up due to thunderstorms, returning the next day, despite manifold risks from Angolan attack helicopters and MiGs, to retrieve the exhausted and injured commandos who were safely, if only narrowly, returned to base. Twelve of the Recce commandos involved in the operation were awarded the Honoris Crux. The Cuito River Bridge, however, was not destroyed but it was severely damaged and was for some time largely unserviceable for heavy traffic. From that point onward helicopter cargo lifts were required to shuttle supplies across the river.

The SAAF, meanwhile, applied itself through photo reconnaissance to gathering as comprehensive a picture of enemy composition and magnitude as possible. For this work Mirage R2Zs were used. It was established that the Angolans were mobile and widely dispersed, comprising tanks, armoured cars and a variety of missile and radar assets. There was little that could be done to influence matters until the two main columns arrived at the Lomba River. The Lomba was close to its headwaters at that point which allowed the 47th Brigade to move around and approach the main bridge crossing from the southern bank with a view to covering the impending crossing by the 59th and 21st brigades. This had the effect of concentrating the various brigade elements on a two-kilometre-wide and softly constituted floodplain which also hindered movement, offering the opportunity for skilful South African gunnery to isolate and begin to deal with the concentration. Air reconnaissance for target selection was provided in large part by a detachment of SAAF RPV (remotely piloted vehicles) aircraft which performed excellent service in identifying targets despite the dense summer foliage. Angolans quickly learned to hate these little aircraft and targeted them with particular malice. Three were brought down by surface-to-air fire, as was a manned Bosbok that was also on an artillery-spotting mission, killing the pilot and artillery officer on board.

On 4 September, 3 Squadron was deployed to AFB Rundu for air-defence duties. At that time the Angolans were flying MiG-23s that could outpace the virtually obsolete but nonetheless irreplaceable SAAF Mirage fleet in straight-line flight. The Angolans also enjoyed superior visibility with the South African radar only able to detect aircraft in the combat area above 24,000 feet thanks to the limits of the radar horizon. The Angolans, on the other hand, with radar emplacements at Cuito Cuanavale and Menongue, enoyed coverage from the ground upward. In some respects, this was like the cliché of taking a knife to a gunfight, but in other respects not. The signature advantage that South African service personnel had enjoyed both on the ground and in the air had been superior leadership, support and training which had succeeded in giving both services a significant edge, and with that in mind, the 3 Squadron pilots waiting patiently in cockpit readiness were supremely confident and anxious to join that elite club of one – Commandant Johan Rankin being the only member thus far – by bagging a MiG. A number of scrambles were ordered but thanks to the distances involved the enemy MiGs had each time left the combat zone by the time the F1s were in position.

On 10 September, however, three pairs of Mirage F1CZs were again scrambled and a short while later Captain Anton van Rensburg indicated that he had visual contact with two MiG-23s. Seconds later, he achieved firing parameters and launched two Matra 550 missiles that both exploded prematurely, allowing both MiGs to slip away and speed back toward Menongue.

In the meanwhile, 1 Squadron arrived at AFB Grootfontein in preparation for the opening sortie of the air operation which was scheduled to kick off on 16 September. By then, South African artillery on the southern bank of the Lomba River had already been modestly successful in knocking out a number of tanks and generally inhibiting, although not halting, the Angolan advance. The air operation was opened with a combined strike against the 47th Brigade, delivering 100 locally modified Mk 82 (250kg)

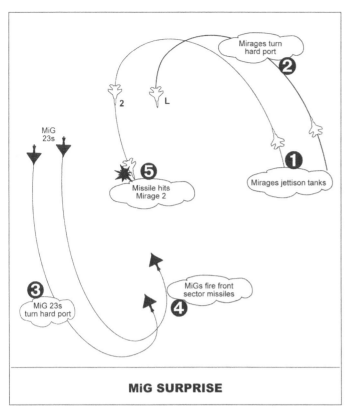

MiG SURPRISE

On 27 September 1987, Captain Arthur Piercy's Mirage FICZ ('Mirage 2' in the diagram) took a missile hit from a MiG-23. 'Mirage L' in the diagram was flown by Carlo Gagiano.

Carlo Gagiano, Piercy's lead.

It was now clear that the enemy now enjoyed a significant technological advantage in the air which could not be countered thanks to the ongoing arms embargo. This left only a re-examination and improvement of tactics to fall back on, after which a certain amount of ad hoc local training was undertaken, but without live fire it remained somewhat theoretical.

pre-fragmentation bombs. Johan Rankin narrowly avoided a multiple missile launch and then, taking stock after a tight evasive manoeuvre, found his tail stirring up the dust of a dry *shona* as he pulled maximum Gs in order to recover before hitting the ground.

Less fortunate was Captain Arthur Piercy who sustained a MiG-23 missile strike in the tail section during a brief dogfight on 27 September. His F1CZ sustained severe damage but thanks to skilled piloting he was able to bring the aircraft in to AFB Rundu. There, however, a lack of hydraulic pressure and a missing drag 'chute caused the Mirage to overshoot the runway which in turn caused the ejection seat to fire and, with insufficient height for the parachute to be effective, Piercy sustained severe and permanent damage to his lower back. This incident curbed the earlier confidence felt among the Mirage pilots and occasioned a pause in *Bellombra* operations while its implications were digested. Lord:

Operation Bellombra was planned to curb this newfound aggression. The idea was to scramble pairs of Mirages to designated low-level holding points whenever MiGs were in the air. Our radar controllers would watch the MiGs and, if they came into the area of one of the holding points, they would give the Mirages a radar vector and time to pitch-up. Our aircraft would accelerate to 600 knots-plus before pitching-up. The idea was to climb to 4,000 feet below the targets. Airborne radar was only switched on during the pitch to give the enemy minimum warning before missile launch was achieved. When our aircraft were detected by Dayton radar they would be vectored onto the bogeys.

Photo reconnaissance and routine ground attacks went on, with the two enemy brigades – the 47th and 21st – eventually breaking. A key battle was fought on 3 October between a mobile SADF force comprising the battle-hardened 61 Mechanized Battalion supported by artillery which, despite having no tanks, took offensive action and almost completely destroyed the FAPLA 47th Brigade, killing some 250 enemy troops. After several weeks of heavy combined airstrikes by Buccaneers, Canberras, Mirages and Impalas, the 3 October battle was a turning point in the offensive, after which the Angolan advance lost all momentum. The much-vaunted 47th Brigade more or less ceased to exist, leaving behind a landscape strewn with stricken armour rendered useless, as much as anything, by the sustained and accurate air delivery of air-bursting pre-fragmented bombs that perforated engines, tyres and radiators, with even serviceable vehicles and tanks eventually being abandoned.

Analysis of the offensive, however, has tended to reveal the dominating role played on the battlefield by South African artillery, in particular using the domestically developed and produced G5 howitzer. The G5, with a range of 40 kilometres, was responsible for much of the damage inflicted on the enemy, hampering the tactical and logistical movement, immobilizing brigades in preparation for SADF mechanized units and UNITA infantry, and later being largely responsible for rendering the all-important airfield at Cuito Cuanavale inoperable. It is also worth noting that the Lomba River battles saw the first operational use of the Olifant main tank.

In the aftermath of the carnage on the Lomba River, the enemy brigades began a long but largely orderly withdrawal back toward Cuito Cuanavale. The Soviets had withdrawn their advisers, leaving FAPLA without senior leadership, and thus the threat to Mavinga and Jamba had been comprehensively neutralized. South African personnel were returned back across the Lomba River on 7 October since, for the time being at least, success had been achieved.

This was not the end of it, however. As Operation *Modular* wound down, Operation *Hooper* commenced, the aim of which was to inflict maximum casualties on the retreating FAPLA forces after they had been halted.

3 Squadron pilots pose formally with their Honorary Colonel. Standing from left: Les Bennett, Mark Raymond, John Sinclair, Rudi Mes, Arthur Piercy, Anton van Rensburg; front from left: Clive Turner, Pierre du Plessis, Carlo Gagiano, Honorary Colonel Pik Botha, Dries Wehmeyer, Johan Barnardt, Pete Cooke.

Angolan FAPA MiG-23.

Two retreating brigades – the 16th and the 21st – had by then been deployed at the source of the Chambinga River, with the 59th Brigade and a tactical group positioned between the Vimpulo and Mianei rivers. Although each had been damaged, they still represented a viable offensive force, and the immediate priority in the aftermath of the withdrawal from the Lomba River was to prevent them from regrouping for another thrust against Mavinga. In order to pre-empt a second offensive in 1988, it was decided, therefore, that the entire Angolan presence east of the Cuito River must be removed.

This was Operation *Packer*, the last of three operations collectively defined as the Battle of Cuito Cuanavale.

For the SAAF, meanwhile, 1987 closed on an interesting note, with the target being the still-standing bridge over the Cuito River, and a rather ground-breaking attempt to bring it down once and for all, making use of a technology that had been present in the South African arsenal for some time and which had been exhaustively tested but never deployed.

The Raptor 1 (H2) glide bomb was a modular system that consisted of the 'glide bomb' itself, a communications pod, usually mounted on the starboard wing opposing the missile mounted on the port wing. Prior to the advent of GPS-assisted inertial navigation, this system utilized a television link between the bomb and the controlling aircraft – this could either be the aircraft delivering the bomb, in which case it would be controlled by the navigator or by a second aircraft not associated with the actual attack. In both instances the weapon was guided to its target using a left-hand joystick in the cockpit, with internal power being supplied to the missile by a generator driven by an impeller located at the rear. The weapon's flight was recorded by means of a video tape recorder mounted in the communications pod. For the purposes of debrief this included the weapon's audio and the crew's intercom conversations as well as the visual sequence filmed from the camera located in the nose of the missile.

The system was adapted for use either by Buccaneers or Impalas, and later Cheetahs, although on the first deployment of the weapon against the Cuito River Bridge on 12 December 1987, during Operation *Modular/Hooper*, it was Buccaneer 414 crewed by pilot Major Pikkie Siebrits and Captain Neil Napier that carried the system. This attack was not completely successful and nor was a follow-up attack carried out on 3 January 1988, although on this run the bridge was damaged sufficiently to further inhibit its practical use.

By late December, meanwhile, FAPLA had begun to attempt to buttress and reinforce its position in and around Cuito Cuanavale, a somewhat more substantial town than was usually found in the region. It was located on the west bank of the Cuito River, a meandering stream with an extensive floodplain and a scattering of pools and small ox-bow lakes. The dropping of the bridge inhibited movement east and then south which, in the short term at least, reduced the risk of a renewed offensive originating from the town, but it did not interfere with logistical and resupply communications stretching back toward Menongue. It was decided, therefore, that interdiction airstrikes would be launched based on intelligence gathered by ground-force reconnaissance teams infiltrated into the area, at great risk to themselves it might added, who then passed back information on the movement of road convoys.

There was considerable reservation expressed by the SAAF during the planning of these operations, bearing in mind that the new theatre of operations which was considerably farther north than the Lomba River, added an addition fuel-capacity advantage to the defending MiGs operating from Menongue, while at the same time handing additional disadvantage to the SAAF Mirages and other aircraft that, with the added flight time needed to get over their targets, were then severely limited in their operational time, perhaps just a few minutes, to complete a mission and deal with any unexpected eventualities. As Brigadier-General Dick Lord put it:

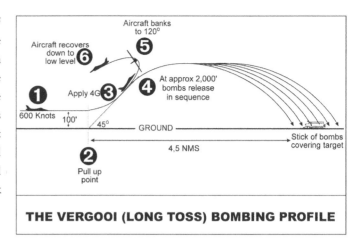

THE VERGOOI (LONG TOSS) BOMBING PROFILE

> The SAAF objections to the plan were based on geography and physical science, not a reluctance to fight. Operation *Moduler* had been fought alongside the Lomba River. On a map it can be seen that the battleground is almost equidistant between Rundu and Menongue. Opposing fighters had to fly approximately the same distance to reach the combat area; therefore, combat fuel allowances for both opponents were similar.[25]

With the battle arena now shifting to an area of high ground east of Cuito Cuanavale, the advantage was yielded almost entirely to the enemy which, alongside basic equipment disparities, certainly gave the Angolans the edge. Fuel differentials, moreover, were simply part of this. Angolan MiGs, with two minutes' flight time from Menongue, were able to fly in clean configuration while the SAAF Mirages, with additional outboard tanks as well as underwing stores, flew into combat in dirty configuration.[26] Angolan and Cuban pilots enjoyed radar cover while the South Africans flew in blind.

In addition, the increase in numbers and sophistication of enemy aircraft also tilted the battlefield against the South Africans, offering the enemy a brief and solitary opportunity to enjoy superiority in the air. Despite all this, the enemy still consistently lost battles, thanks in large part to superior SAAF airmanship, meticulous planning and exhaustive training.

Low-level flight and navigation tended to characterize operations throughout the various phases of the offensive, with a low-level toss-bomb (*vergooi*) delivery profile being used. This tactic involved pitching the aircraft up around four nautical miles from the objective and literally 'tossing' the bombs toward the target. This was perfected with the use of finely tuned on-board computer systems and weapons specifically designed for the prevailing military situation in Angola.

The interdiction operations flown against the huge road convoys moving between Menongue and Cuito Cuanavale usually took place at last light or at dawn during that happy moment before enemy aircraft could expect to be encountered and while sufficient light was still available. These were consistent and ongoing operations, the details for which were usually handed over the night before, requiring pilots to undertake pre-flight planning late into the evening, waking then in the early hours to

take to the air and head north. The year-end hazard of the 'big rains' also complicated and hampered operations, with the only advantage being that in thick cloud and low visibility the danger from anti-aircraft defences on the ground was minimal.

It was not enemy MiGs, however, nor AAA that posed the greatest practical danger, but the ubiquitous Strela SAM-7. During this concluding seven months of the war a total of 683 Mirage combat sorties were flown, delivering nearly 4,000 bombs and it is estimated that during this period more than 100 surface-to-air missiles were launched against them.[27]

Offensive operations paused briefly as 1988 dawned for the prosaic reason that the South African national service changeover required new intakes of conscripted troops to replace those completing their national service at the front, who were in turn heading back to civilian life in South Africa. Matters resumed soon afterward, however, when tragic proof was given of the vulnerability of SAAF aircraft to Angolan air defences when F1AZ 245, the only Mirage F1 to be brought down in combat, was shot down near Cuito Cuanavale during a *vergooi* mission against a significant road convoy moving on the Menongue–Cuito Cuanavale road.

The incident occurred during the early afternoon of 20 February when a four-ship formation took off to follow up on information passed back by a 32 Battalion reconnaissance team. The same area had seen a number of sorties flown and enemy anti-aircraft defences were on high alert. After releasing his bombs, Major Edward Every was hit at low altitude and crashed shortly afterward. Because no emergency calls had been picked up or any activity registered from the pilot's PELBA beacon it was assumed that Every had been killed.

It was concluded after a thorough analysis of the episode that the mission had simply been one too many over that particular location, presenting the enemy with an opportunity to study the SAAF tactics in that particular situation and then ensuring that an air-defence battery was in position for a repeat of earlier operations. After the bomb release and as Every broke off, the missile system locked onto the F1's exhaust plume, successfully tracking and striking it as it reached low level.

The SAAF at all times sought to avoid predictability, with this sad episode proving the undeniable wisdom of that. A comprehensive search and rescue was immediately launched in the vain hope that an emergency radio transmission would be picked up. In the end, the inevitable was conceded, with salt being applied to the wound by the display in Luanda some time later of the wreckage of Major Every's aircraft. Every's death, the last SAAF fatality of the war, was felt very keenly among the compact community of SAAF Mirage pilots.

Two days prior to Every's death a determined airstrike was aimed at Lubango, the largest combined FAPLA and SWAPO HQ in the region, inflicting serious damage on two facilities. These were the Tobias Hanyeko Training Centre, SWAPO's most important training and military facility, and an insurgent holding camp located about ten kilometres outside the city. This was a daring attack, bearing in mind how the city bristled with anti-aircraft defences, and there was a touch of bravado in it.

A terror bombing in Oshakati, northern South West Africa, had recently claimed the lives of 20 civilians, with SWAPO attempting the ridiculous claim that the incident had been staged by the South Africans. It has been suggested that the strike had the twin of a reprisal for the Oshakati bombing and to bring it home to the Angolans that the South Africans were still very much in the fight.

In the meanwhile, two short and sharp dogfights took place a few days later when two sorties were intercepted by MiG-23s. In the first of these Major Willie van Coppenhagen and captains David Kleynhans and Reg van Eeden turned to fight, upon which the MiGs promptly broke away and fled.

On the second sortie Commandant Rankin alongside Major Frans Coetzee and Captain Trompie Nel were warned that they were being stalked by a Cuban MiG-23. Enemy radio frequencies were being monitored with the help of a Spanish-speaking interpreter who inferred from descriptions exchanged of the Mirage camouflage that the Cubans had the South Africans visual. Rankin immediately ordered the F1 pilots to drop their fuel

tanks and broke into the rapidly approaching MiGs at precisely the correct range. Rankin saw two MiGs flash overhead and manoeuvred into position behind them. However, both aircraft and weapons were outdistanced by the fast-moving enemy aircraft and the moment was lost.

Rankin concluded that part of the problem had been that the Mirage camouflage was too easy to spot and took a somewhat risky personal decision to alter it overnight in the hangar, which might have resulted in court martial but in fact ended in a general re-evaluation of the Mirage livery. A project was then registered to develop a camouflage pattern that was better suited to the Mirage F1AZ in its various roles. Aircraft 243 was painted dark blue underneath and dark brown and green above. On 2 March 1988 1 Squadron was stood down from operations and all aircraft flown back to AFB Hoespruit. There, as an interim measure, they were officially modified to a dark-earth and matt-green colour scheme.

Six F1AZs were returned to AFB Grootfontein from AFB Hoedspruit on 19 March, two of which were used for a *Donkermaan* diversionary strike on an area target near the town of Longa, more or less midway between Monnow and Cuito Cuanavale. In marginal weather conditions the two pilots, Commandant Johan Rankin and Major Willie van Coppenhagen, maintained radio silence and a loose flying formation. Upon return, van Coppenhagen's aircraft crashed, possibly due to a corroded fuel line which might have caused the F1's engine to flame out at low altitude, killing the pilot and prompting a massive search and rescue that established within a few days the site of the accident and the fact the van Coppnehagen had not survived.

The last Mirage sortie of the war was flown on 23 March. The operation was intended as a *vergooi* attack at 100 feet but was aborted because of deteriorating weather conditions.

Two days later the squadron was stood down and returned to AFB Hoedspruit.

CHAPTER ELEVEN:
PEACE, DISENGAGEMENT AND INDEPENDENCE

On the battlefield events were similarly winding down. The highly complex political manoeuvring that had been underway throughout the combined seven months of operations *Modular*, *Hooper* and *Packer* had been salutary for all sides. The South Africans had, through the introduction of the G5 and G6 artillery systems and, of course, the Olifant main tank, inched the war a little further toward a full-scale conventional confrontation; the offensive, in fact, still ranks as the largest land battle fought on African soil since El Alamein and the only set-piece conventional armoured confrontation in sub-Saharan Africa to ever use tanks in their correct mobile role. What was to be the next step?

South Africa could entertain a very slim hope of ever closing the technical gap that was widening in the air war with the arrival in the theatre of the latest MiG-23s, besides which, what, beyond

demilitarizing southern Angola for her own protection, could South Africa hope to tactically achieve by an advanced military agenda?

From the point of view of the Angolan/Cuban/Soviet troika, South Africa – even though, as many high-ranking military planners and observers had noted, had entered the ring blind and with one hand tied behind her back – had still delivered the combined forces of the enemy such a profound beating that the notion of engaging in a third offensive seemed distinctly unattractive. Statistics are obviously always unreliable in circumstances such as this but an analysis of many sources suggests enemy personnel killed or wounded in this series of operations run to over 4,000, with hundreds of logistic vehicles, armoured fighting vehicles, aircraft, tanks and allied missile and

Alouette III 634 over Pretoria.

A 17 Squadron Puma banks over Waterkloof.

radar systems, tens of millions of dollars' worth, possibly more, destroyed or captured by the South Africans. The South Africans, on the other hand, lost a total of 40 men killed, 114 wounded, with three armoured fighting vehicles and three tanks lost.

In terms of the propaganda war, it need hardly be said that South Africa was the loser, particularly since the diplomatic necessity of a blanket news silence covering the entire episode left the battlefield entirely open to the enemy to exploit, which it did. However, if South Africa was running out of breath in the long haul, then the allied enemy front, supported in one way or another entirely by Soviet largess and commitment, was stumbling even more noticeably as the countdown to the end of communist rule in Eastern Europe began.

This, however, also undermined much of South Africa's claim to be standing alone against the communist 'total onslaught' since, if communism as a global ideology effectively ceased to exist then the *raison d'être* for South African intervention in Angola disappeared with it. All that might remain at the bottom of the crucible would be a congenital reluctance to witness South West African independence for no better reason than racism.

As far as the MPLA and UNITA were concerned, increasing oil revenues in Angola gradually began to replace Cold War patronage as the fuel of war, a war that would continue in one form or another until Savimbi's death in action in 2002. A separate peace initiative between these two parties was attempted by Zairean President Mobuto Sese Seko and, although a token understanding was reached, there would be no respite in this particular conflict for some time to come. The US ramped up its aid to UNITA in the aftermath of the Namibian peace, with the melancholy result that by 1990 an estimated 100,000 lives had been sacrificed with a further 900,000 people facing famine.

This, however, did not intrude in the short term on the most optimum conditions for peace in the region since the onset of the generation-long Border War. In April 1988 the Soviet Union and Cuba finally bent to the long-standing American and South African demand for 'linkage', this being the withdrawal of Cuban troops from Angola as part of a package for Namibian independence. A number of meetings were then held throughout the remainder of 1988 as the two sides sought a practical formula which in due

course was drafted into an agreement signed in New York on 22 December 1988. Under the terms of this agreement the 50,000 or so Cuban troops stockpiled in Angola during the course of the conflict would be withdrawn in stages, concluding in July 1991. South Africa agreed to implement UN Resolution 435 leading to Namibian independence in 1990. Moreover, all South African forces would be withdrawn upon a minimum of conditions, one being the similar withdrawal from Angola of some 10,000 ANC militants purported to be in-country.

The opening months of 1989 saw the beginning of a huge operation to pack up and return a 23-year military establishment back to South Africa. By the end of March of that year, some 260 trainloads of arms, ammunition, armour and vehicles of every description had left the border area en route for bases and depots across South Africa. While all this was underway, SAAF airfield maintenance units upgraded and refurbished UNITA's runways at Jamba and Liuana as a valedictory gesture in what would be the closing chapter of a lengthy saga of mutual reliance. Also in March the first United Nations Transition Assistance Group (UNTAG) arrivals began to make their appearance, those that would form the interim authority in the region and scheduled to assume authority on 1 April 1989.

This, for all intents and purposes, was the end, but was it? Those realists and cynics among the many observers anticipated, and were not surprised by, an effort by SWAPO to make use of the general feeling of goodwill and a lapse of vigilance in order to launch what was reckoned to be the infiltration of the largest PLAN force into South West Africa thus far. This was clearly an attempt to seize the country by force rather than submit itself to the risky potential of a UN-monitored free and fair election.

There is, of course, another version of the nine-day running fight that took place between the PLAN detachment numbering some 1,500 heavily armed combatants and a similar number of SWATF policemen, many among them members of the elite counter-insurgency unit Koevoet, assisted by SAAF Alouette III helicopter gunships.[28] This version, published on behalf of the European Union, a body very frequently guilty of grasping at any nugget of notoriety from the many that South Africa had to offer, claimed that these fighters, carrying nothing but goodwill alongside their heavy burdens of RPG-7s, mortars, landmines and other terror equipment, merely sought the opportunity to hand in their weapons and integrate themselves into the democratic process.[29] This may quite possibly have been so, as might have been the saintly portrayal of Sam Nujoma who no doubt authorized the incursion, although the reality of liberation politics in Africa would strongly suggest otherwise. Whatever might have been the truth, while the politicians pointed fingers the fighting men fought and died.

On 31 March South West African Police patrols first noticed the spoor of a large body of heavily burdened men crossing the cut-line and moving inland into Owamboland where, incidentally, the first action of the insurgency had taken place a quarter of a century earlier. Under the terms of Resolution 435 SADF personnel remaining in South West Africa were confined to base, which presented some difficulties, but a plan to confront the insurgency was hastily devised using local South West African forces and codenamed Operation *Merlyn*.

The crossing had taken place at four different points, the extremes of which were 300 kilometres apart. One column entered just east of Ruacana and another split into two groups at Oshikango and advanced thereafter toward Oshakati and Ondangwa. Another two-pronged incursion entered the country west of Nkongo, with one group heading for the white farming area around Namutoni and the other moving toward Kavango.

The first contact took place on the morning of 1 April 1989 on the day that the ceasefire officially came into effect. Helicopters were slow to get involved, mainly, it was suggested by Brigadier-General Lord, that the Alouette crews believed that the call-out was an April Fools' prank and did not take it seriously. However, upon arriving over the scene and achieving visual contact with a large group of insurgents, authority to open fire was denied. This was extremely frustrating for the crews, but even more so for the SWAPOL liaison crew who sat in the helicopter orbiting the target with no coercion whatsoever being enough to goad the SAAF gunner to open fire. No small amount of inter-service commentary would have circulated that day as elements of lightly armed SWAPOL took on the insurgents with the SAAF doing nothing at all to help. This was no less frustrating for the SAAF men but it is testimony to their discipline and training that orders were not disobeyed. By the end of day one of Operation *Merlyn*, however, some 130 PLAN insurgents and ten SWAPOL details were dead.

Heavy fighting then spread across a 300-kilometre front with civilian refugees converging on Oshakati and Ongwediva. On 2 April there were 30 contacts in which 42 insurgents were killed for the loss of four SWAPOL members. The political fallout of the incident, as can be imagined, was intense. South African Foreign Minister Pik Botha issued a stringent complaint to UN Secretary-General Xavier Perez de Cuellar which found its way to Sam Nujoma attending an international parliamentarians' conference in Harare, where a series of shrill, contradictory and patently untrue statements were issued in reply. Besides this, there

Casspir and Aloette III, a deadly Koevoet–SAAFcombination.
Photo Leon Bezuidenhout

Mounted 120mm gun and MAG on a Koevoet vehicle.
Photo Leon Bezuidenhout

Koevoet in action during the PLAN's 1 April invasion.
Photo Leon Bezuidenhout

was a great deal of hand-wringing and emergency debating that continued throughout the nine days of the operation. Alouettes were rushed back to the border in the holds of C-160s, assembled, tested and sent into the fight. Eight Honoris Crux were awarded to various aircrew flying reconnaissance, casualty evacuation and troop deployments, evading a concerted effort by the enemy to bring them down, and at all times remaining true to the letter of

A Koevoet vehicle falls prey to a PLAN landmine.
Photo Leon Bezuidenhout

Koevoet POMZ casualties. POMZs and landmines were the principal causes of Koevoet casualties. *Photo Leon Bezuidenhout*

the ceasefire agreement while SWAPOL reacted largely unaided as the civil authority.

During the course of the operation, 750 insurgents were killed or wounded, more than half the original force, while 22 security force members died. In addition, 21 Casspir and Ratel fighting vehicles were hit by RPG-7 rockets. The brunt of the fighting was done by Koevoet but the local Owambo 101 Battalion was also reintroduced to assist.

The SAAF MAOT at Eenhana called out an Impala strike to just west of the base to assist a hard-pressed Koevoet stick, firing salvos of rockets into SWAPO defence lines. In general, the SAAF contribution had been heliborne with ships from 16 and 17 squadrons involved, operating from the Ondangwa, Eenhana and Ruacana bases. By day four of the operation, a total of 15 Pumas and 22 Alouette helicopters were operational.

There is a certain poetry in the fact that SAAF helicopter crews

were in at the beginning and the end but there certainly seemed to be a great deal of unnecessary bloodshed considering that peace had already been negotiated. However, what cannot be denied and what perhaps is fitting as a last comment in this narrative is that the courage displayed by the PLAN units involved in the incursion, whatever might have been the mindset of their political handlers, was more frequently than not above reproach. In fact, many of the PLAN incursions were similarly undertaken by extraordinarily valorous men, with more attention than is perhaps fair being given to the SADF and associated security forces for the skill with which these men were tracked down, run to ground and killed. This is true, but it takes a particular type of courage and commitment to set off in the direction of almost certain death in the furtherance of an agenda that had about it all the Orwellian attributes that the 21st century has revealed in the African revolution. Another point worthy of ending upon.

APPENDIX:
ACCOUNT OF AN MAOT OFFICER DURING OPERATION *ASKARI* BY CAPTAIN CHARLIE WROTH

On a Friday afternoon, early in November 1983, Spof Fee, Russell Espley-Jones and I landed our C-130 at AFB Waterkloof and made our way to the officers' mess for drinks. Here we discovered that one of us was required for a two-month ground tour on the border. Being the youngest I was 'volunteered'. I flew out on Sunday morning to AFB Grootfontein where I learned I was to be the MAOT with 61 Mechanized Battalion during Operation *Askari*.

At AFB Grootfontein I was issued with a specially equipped command Ratel, an armoured fighting vehicle nicknamed 'Asterix'. My team consisted of my army driver, 'Herman von Fochville', Citizen Force Corporal Paul from Stellenbosch University and a flight sergeant radio operator ex-Rhodesian Air Force. The command vehicle used by SAAF differed from the Ratel used by the army in two ways: a) the SAAF vehicle had no

armaments and b) the rear section of the SAAF Ratel was filled with mattresses.

After crossing the cut-line at Oshikango, 61 Mech headed toward Ongiva. En route the army commander exercised his unit by shouting "*Visgraat!*" over the radio. This term was used when enemy MiGs were in the vicinity to rapidly disperse the armoured column: vehicles turn off the road, alternately left and right, to park under the cover of the nearest suitable tree. The Afrikaans word translates to 'fishbone' and is very appropriate. The reaction appears chaotic but it worked. Within seconds the 100-vehicle convoy had disappeared. However, getting the column reorganized turned out to be quite a mission.

We continued north from Ongiva toward Mupa, our first target. The attack was led by Ratel 90s, supported by mortar fire and accompanied by psychological warfare loudspeakers belting

'Asterix', the SAAF MAOT Ratel on *Operation Askari*. Charlie Wroth wears the beard.

The captured SA-9 missile system.

out the theme tune for *The Green Berets*. The town was taken in a surreal atmosphere, my first impression that it was something out of the *Kelly's Heroes* movie. Normality returned when two Alouettes piloted by Carl Alberts and Mike Fagin rendezvoused with the battle group. Sleeping out under the Angolan stars was a new experience for the SAAF. Everyone had to dig their own slit trench to sleep in. Once again, the difference between the browns and the blues was obvious: each SAAF trench had a mattress in it.

The battalion stopped in Xangongo to regroup, giving me the opportunity to see the damaged caused to buildings during Operation *Protea*, targets of AS-30 missiles fired from my Buccaneer. Operating off Xangongo airstrip were two SAAF Pumas, two Alouettes, a Bosbok and a team flying the RPV.

In Xangongo I met a group of soldiers who had found the wreckage of the SAAF Canberra shot down on 14 March 1979. They had organized the digging of a deep trench and had buried the remains of the aircraft. I was touched by this deed as Second Lieutenant Owen Doyle who was killed in the crash had been my roommate in the SAAF and we had attended Grey College in Port Elizabeth together.

From Xangongo we moved west on our mission to capture a Soviet SAM-8 missile system near Ediva. At this stage Major Dudley Wall was allocated to my vehicle. I was never quite sure of his mission, nevertheless we became good friends. After approximately three days, we launched an attack near Ediva but were met by Soviet T-54 tanks and BRDM armoured cars, well supported by their mortars. A number of our Ratels had wheels knocked out and a Unimog took a mortar in the back. Casualties were suffered and the attack was called off. While recovering injured soldiers from damaged vehicles, the medics took serious shrapnel wounds in their backs and were later decorated for bravery under fire. Light was starting to fade but I called in a Puma to casevac the injured. Escorted by two Ratel 60s, I set up an LZ in a disued quarry. Light was fading fast and the Puma called for white phos (phosphorus grenades) so they could locate the LZ as they were looking straight into the setting sun. With great caution I pulled the pin from the grenade and threw it farther than I have ever thrown a cricket ball. Captain Steel Upton landed

the Puma and the medics, after stabilizing one of the seriously wounded soldiers, loaded the injured and the helicopter took off for Ondangwa. Sadly, we learned that the soldiers passed away during the flight.

61 Mech then repositioned northeast of Cahama and spent a week in the bush moving between Cahama and Chibemba. (One of the principles of war is that of manoeuvre; this is what 61 Mech was busy with. No commander enjoys having his enemy moving around his flank or manoeuvring in his rear.) On either Christmas Day or the day after, one of our Ratel 90s detonated a triple landmine. The blast split the vehicle's shell and burned the men inside from the top down. However, although they were all as black as night, they were casevaced out and survived. The casevac helicopter brought in General Constand Viljoen for a quick flying visit even though we were 350 kilometres inside Angola.

The next day we set up an ambush on the road between Lubango and Cahama. A military Mercedes truck drove into the ambush and was shot up. Everybody on board was killed except for an Irish nurse. I was asked to fly her out but due to the lateness of the day this was not possible. She spent the night with a Special Forces unit. The next day when I briefed her on helicopter boarding drills, she said there was no need because she already knew the drill: the SADF had ambushed her vehicle exactly a year before.

The ambush was re-set and an Angolan reconnaissance team investigating the still-smouldering vehicle entered the killing zone. There was a lot of whispering on the radios trying to confirm they were not our troops when suddenly all hell broke loose. "*Gat toe, gat toe!*" (To the trenches, to the trenches) was yelled as we all dived into our slit trenches, even the SAAF personnel. Two RPGs were fired in our direction, one exploding against a tree right behind us and the other self-destructing a bit farther away. My deafness lasted quite a few days. Once again, our troops managed to get the upper hand and destroyed the enemy recce team. The Angolan team leader was buried in a shallow grave next to my Ratel.

At midnight on Christmas Day the Canberras bombed Cahama. To ease their night bombing problem we fired white phos shells in a line leading to their target. Using my MAOT radio, I was able to exchange Christmas greetings with Dave Knoesen, the leader

The bridge at Xangongo.

Knoesen and Wroth.

of the Canberra formation. We had flown together as a Buccaneer crew; now he was at 24,000 feet and I was getting 'stonked' on the ground. The lesson we learned that night was when you fire artillery you give away your position to the enemy and Cahama retaliated very accurately.

Our vehicles took a severe pounding as we bundu-bashed through the veld. Here I have to give praise to the army echelon support crews and the tiffies (mechanics) who maintained our vehicles and kept our logistic supply going. Our 'Asterix' required their attention after we hit a low-hanging branch over the road and our turret went through a snap 90-degree turn. Fortunately, we were all out of the turret or it would have cut us in half. While our Ratel was being repaired by a tiffie, 61 Mech was on the move, so we were towed by another Ratel.

61 Mech was then tasked to return in great haste through Xangongo to Cuvelai to lend support to our other battle group engaged there. During this long drive the armoured column stopped in line astern to celebrate New Year's Day. We did this by firing a burst of tracer simultaneously from all the Ratels toward the north, a very different fireworks display from the ones we all grew up with. We moved north toward Cuvelai and positioned ourselves southeast of the town. The weather was low cloud and rain. The battle for Cuvelai took place on 4 January. Our approach

to the town was hindered by a defensive minefield. Some of our Ratels detonated mines and one was hit by a 76mm shell from the side, our single biggest loss as ten guys were killed.

We learned from our experience at Cuvelai that all Angolan towns were surrounded by minefields. What the enemy did was clear the area of bush after cutting the trunks about a metre off the ground then plant the field with *muhango* (sorghum). This hid the stumps which were the right height to sever the hydraulics and brake lines underneath our vehicles.

Once we took the town, we appropriately made ourselves comfortable in the blue house which until a few hours before had been the home of the Soviet commissar. We parked our Ratel in the dining room and set up our communications. We could see the previous occupants had left in a hurry as suitcases had been packed but not taken. The flag which we took off the flagpole is still in my possession as my memento of *Askari*.

To the west of the runway we found a complete SA-9 missile system, a *boeretroos*, or sop, for not getting the SA-8, our main prize. After the town was secured, many people, including members of the press, were flown in for a media briefing. For us it was the end of the operation. I had spent two months in Angola and travelled 3,500 kilometres in a Ratel. As MAOT I had sent back 21 body bags and 54 serious casevacs.

Notes

1   Arguably the most famous of these was Arthur 'Bomber' Harris who lived in both Rhodesia and South Africa and rose to the leadership of the RAF Bomber Command during the Second World War.

2   A *draadkar*, or wire car, is a homemade car toy played with traditionally by black children in southern Africa, and is an ingenious construction of wire and other oddments with an extended steering wheel allowing it to be driven along at a walking or running pace by its driver.

3   Thanks for this information to Paul Dubois published on *www.sa-transport.co.za*.

4   Crocker, Chester. *High Noon in Africa: Making Peace in a Rough Neighbourhood*, Jonathan Ball, Johannesburg, 1992, p. 46.

5   Both Alpha and Bravo comprised companies of indigenous troops, in the first instance drawn from elements of the FLNA inducted into the SADF, and in the second by Angolan Bushmen who had suffered significant attrition at the hands of each of the Angolan warring parties at one time or other, and who were at the very least an enigmatic force in the conflic

6   Stiff, Peter. *The Silent War: South African Recce Operations 1969–1994*, Galago, Johannesburg, 1999, pp. 120–1.

7   The alpha bomb was a Rhodesian Air Force innovation conceived and developed by Group Captain Peter Petter-Bowyer. It was a spherical bouncing bomb with a delayed detonation allowing for the airburst of multiple fragments over a wide area. The system was configured for deployment from Rhodesian Canberra bombers and was adopted and improved upon for similar use in the South African-operated Canberras

8   ZIPRA, or the Zimbabwe People's Revolutionary Army, was the armed wing of ZAPU, the Zimbabwe African People's Union, one of two armed factions attempting the overthrow of white rule in Rhodesia.

9   Steenkamp, Willem. *South Africa's Border War: 1966–1989*, Ashanti, Gibraltar, 1989, p. 86.

10 ZANLA, or the Zimbabwe African National Liberation Army, was the armed wing of ZANU, one of two nationalist factions fighting to overthrow white rule in Rhodesia.

11 MAOTs were SAAF teams usually comprising an OC (pilot), an operations officer, an intelligence officer, a radio operator and one or two clerks. Teams and equipment were typically airlifted into a tactical HQ co-located with the army or police or in a mobile situation as part of a motorized column as part of the command HQ. The MAOT acted as an advisory to a field commander regarding close air support as operations progressed, interpreting highly dynamic conditions on the ground into practical air support operations. (See appendix for a firsthand account of an MAOT on Operation *Askari*)

12 The AS-30 was a short-to-medium-range air-to-ground missile that used MCLOS (manual command to line of sight) guidance. This required the pilot or gunner to steer the missile to target through a UHF radio link with the missile and typically a left-handed joystick, using a magnesium flare at the base of the missile as a visual reference. Pinpoint accuracy was marginal and a high level of concentration was required for effective targeting.

13 Steenkamp, Willem. *South Africa's Border War: 1966–1989*, Ashanti, Gibraltar, 1989, p. 98.

14 Cockpit standby implies a state of readiness whereby the pilot is fully equipped and on standby in flight position. This was under shelter usually thanks to the punishing heat of the South West African summer.

15 Fire Force is an airborne assault concept pioneered in the region by the Rhodesian security forces and further developed by South Africa. Its model application involves a highly mobile response force equipped with helicopters and supported by paratroops on permanent standby to respond to intelligence provided either by pseudo or covert reconnaissance missions within an active area.

16 Lord, Brig-Gen Dick. *From Fledgling to Eagle: The South African Air Force during the Border War*, 30 Degrees South, Johannesburg, 2008, p. 232.

17 Lord, Brig-Gen Dick. *From Fledgling to Eagle: The South African Air Force during the Border War*, 30 Degrees South, Johannesburg, 2008, p. 290.

18 Arguably the most famous of these is Etosha Pan, situated in north/central Namibia and part of the Etosha Pan National Park. Similar features are scattered throughout the region and may be as small as a few dozen metres across or as expansive as Etosha Pan which is 120km long at its widest girth.

19 Volcano was a SWAPO Special Force/commando unit trained to a higher degree than most PLAN combatants, with individuals referring to themselves as Typhoon comrades. This group infiltrated SWA in

1983 and were dealt with in Operation *Phoenix* of that same year.

20 Lord, Brig-Gen Dick. *From Fledgling to Eagle: The South African Air Force during the Border War*, 30 Degrees South, Johannesburg, 2008, p. 305.

21 Lord, Brig-Gen Dick. *From Fledgling to Eagle: The South African Air Force during the Border War*, 30 Degrees South, Johannesburg, 2008, p. 309.

22 Jamba, Cuando Cubango Province (distinct from Jamba in Huíla Province) is situated in the southeastern corner of Angola, more or less equidistant between Rundu and Katima Mulilo in Nambia and therefore very close to the centre of South African operations.

23 By 1984, the regional coverage by Soviet-supplied radar systems located in Mozambique, Zimbabwe, Zambia and Angola fairly comprehensively blanketed the region in overlapping spheres. However, between Cuito Cuanavale in Angola and Mulobezi in Zambia a narrow gap of coverage existed that allowed SAAF aircraft to slip behind enemy lines more or less at will. In order for that gap to be closed it was necessary for the town of Mavinga to be liberated from UNITA control, which in large part was why the battle for that town was so consistent and so hard-fought.

24 The CIA and South Africa seldom, if ever, overlapped in their support of UNITA. To quote southern African military historian Peter Stiff from his exhaustive study of South African reconnaissance operations, *The Silent War*: "Cooperation between the CIA and the SADF was at arm's length. There was no joint planning of operations in support of UNITA. In fact, like suitors in a love triangle, both competed for UNITA's favours."

25 Lord, Brig-Gen Dick. *From Fledgling to Eagle: The South African Air Force during the Border War*, 30 Degrees South, Johannesburg, 2008, p. 426.

26 The clean/dirty configuration in aviation parlance implies a minimum of drag experienced with undercarriage lifted, no outboard tanks and no underwing armaments: clean configuration. Conversely, with various accoutrements attached to an aircraft when fully loaded, with weapons and fuel tanks included, increased drag in flight, inhibiting manoeuvrability and implying disadvantage: dirty configuration.

27 Dubois, Paul, *Mirage F1 in SAAF Service*, www.sa-transport.co.za.

28 Koevoet, known officially as the South West African Police Counter-Insurgency Unit (SWAPOL-COIN), was a counter-insurgency unit operational during the 1970s and 1980s. The majority of the members were native Namibians. The unit was disbanded soon after this incident. *Koevoet* translates in the Afrikaans as a 'crowbar'.

29 Torreguitar, Elena, *National Liberation Movements in Office: Forging Democracy with African Adjectives in Namibia*, Peter Lang, Frankfurt, 2009, p. 138.

Thanks

The author and the publishers would like to extend a special thank-you to William Marshall who produced the fine aircraft colour profiles that appear in the colour section of this book. William also supplied all the colour photographs in this section.

Peter Baxter is an author, amateur historian and African field, mountain and heritage travel guide. Born in Kenya and educated in Zimbabwe, he has lived and travelled over much of southern and central Africa. He has guided in all the major mountain ranges south of the equator, helping develop the concept of sustainable travel, and the touring of battlefield and heritage sites in East Africa. Peter lives in Oregon, USA, working on the marketing of African heritage travel as well as a variety of book projects. His interests include British Imperial history in Africa and the East Africa campaign of the First World War in particular. His first book was *Rhodesia: Last Outpost of the British Empire*; he has written several books in the Africa@War series, including *France in Centrafrique*, *Selous Scouts*, *Mau Mau* and *SAAF's Border War*.

Lightning Source UK Ltd.
Milton Keynes UK
UKOW06f0400100115

244259UK00007B/30/P